A Child's Legacy

September 11th 2001, the Remaking of America

Bill Geringswald

PublishAmerica
Baltimore

First printing

ISBN: 1-59286-244-6
PUBLISHED BY PUBLISHAMERICA BOOK PUBLISHERS
www.publishamerica.com
Baltimore

Printed in the United States of America

For my great-grandchildren and my mother, whom they will never know.

While it has taken me many years to bring this book into its present reality, I want to thank Carol Givner, Crickett Bardwell, Clay Sutton, and my brothers, Richard and Dan, for their editing and reading expertise. They have made this a much better product than I could have hoped for. I also want to thank the personnel at PublishAmerica for giving this first time writer a chance.

September 11th 2001 … "the day the unimaginable became the imaginable"
-larry sinclair-a good guide if you are ever lost

All errors are mine.

IMAGINE if we could shrink the Earth's population to a village of precisely 100 people. With the entire existing human ratio remaining a constant, it would be demographically described as the following:

There would be:

57 Asians

21 Europeans

14 from the Western Hemisphere, North, Central and the South Americas combined.

8 would be Africans

52 female

70 would be non-white

30 would be Caucasian

70 would be non-Christian

89 would be heterosexual

11 homosexual

6 people would possess and control 59% of the World's entire wealth. All would be from the United States.

80 of this village population would live in substandard housing

70 would be unable to read or write

50 would suffer from malnutrition and 1 would be near death

1 would be near birth

1 would have a computer and

1 with a college education

When one considers this world from such a compressed perspective, the need for compassionate human understanding becomes glaringly apparent. If you have food in the refrigerator, clothes on your back and a sheltered place to sleep, you are richer than 75% of the world. If you woke up this morning with more health than illness, you are doing better than a million others who will die this week.

If you have money in the bank and spare change in a dish, you are among the top 8% of the worlds wealthy. If you can attend a church without fear of harassment, arrest, torture, or death, you are more blessed than 3 billion people in the world. If you have never experienced the danger of battle, the agony of torture, imprisonment, or starvation, you are ahead of 500 million others in the world. And if your parents are still alive and still married to their original spouse, you are very rare, even in this country.

If you can hold someone's hand, hug him or her; you are blessed because you can offer a healing touch. If you hold up your head with a smile on your face and are truly thankful, you are blessed because most do not. As you read this and are reminded of the world's realities, remember just how blessed we really are, living in the United States.

Author unknown – samwel@www.tribute.creoletechnologies.com

INTRODUCTION

God did not intend human life to be this difficult or dangerous. Or, at times, so overwhelming. We question why the One who created All allows so many disasters to happen around us. We are rarely inclined to look at ourselves as the larger cause.

I started writing *A Child's Legacy* in my mind, 26 years ago, using the above as my premise. A newspaper article I read, while waiting for a connecting flight in Memphis, TN, then marked me with a larger perspective of how fragile and unintentionally unaware we are as a human race. For some reason, even now not easily explained, this report struck me deeply with an ominous intuitive feeling. I do not want to be interpreted as a harbinger of an impending doom in this discourse, but my internal senses were then, and still are, involuntarily tightening; presenting me with a silent yet screaming message that we are unintentionally in the midst of creating massive, irreparable damage to ourselves and our mutual home.

The global carnage portrayed in this dated article presented a dismal social and ecological picture. It left little in the way of any hope that we had a chance to repair the damage that we had inflicted upon this Earth. I thought at the time that if we lose the integrity of our life systems, then all that we think, say and do, and all the money we have in the bank is going to be totally meaningless.

It wasn't that I hadn't heard these projections concerning the ecology and our societal problems before. I read the *Smithsonian* and *National Geographic* and today, catch the CNN and PBS Channels for my edification. But something then, perhaps the timing or the particular narrative used, hit me as the intuitive proverbial hammer. I think you know what I mean when this happens to us, with our subconscious sensing that something bad is about to transpire. This seems to be our animal instinct for our personal survival; something strikes our inner awareness telling us that something really bad is about to happen … something that could be life threatening.

Oftentimes, I find that this internal alarm is nothing more than our wild imaginations rising to our conscious brains. We shake off the moment with a silent breathlessness, a major inhale glad to still be alive.

As with many other things in our lives, the impact of that moment, was shelved to the demands of the time, placed on the backburner to other important issues like my financial survival. The incident of September 11th 2001 brought this article's message back into my current consciousness, awakening me to our growing insanities and present emotional damage we are needlessly doing to ourselves.

Since the events of that September morning I am, once again, realizing that our lives are here for a bigger reason that I did not understand almost three decades ago. My mental instincts are now telling me to start looking at and become aware of the much larger picture — hence this writing.

Although I am not a history buff, I have been educated to realize that many of the Earth's past great civilizations advanced to a certain point on the evolutionary scale and then some outside force arose and caused them to implode. I can also believe that a certain part of their populations sensed that something was going very wrong, long before their unseen downfalls. They probably had a gnawing and uncomfortable internal feeling that things were not as they were supposed to be, but couldn't quite get a clear picture of the cause.

They may have tried to discuss their internal concerns with some of their friends and family members but didn't know where to turn, or the proper words to use. They were probably, like us, caught up in their day-to-day pressures, their personal problems, seemingly oblivious to the events surrounding their lives. They were trusting that someone or something would happen to reverse what their circumstances were telling them. Apparently there was no one around who was truly listening, as all are empty shells of what they once were; the most powerful nations of the Earth in their times. Their many opportunities for advancement and tenure inadvertently lost to outside forces, or casually thrown away.

A business associate told me not too long ago that a man has to reach the age of 50 to start paying attention, to appreciate things other than personal gratification and work. Because of my passing into this age threshold, that little light bulb finally went off in my head, awakening me from what seems my past slumber. I have found that I have been a slow learner in this arena as it is only now, almost three decades later from those few idle moments spent with that newspaper, that I have a level of hope to understand the extent and eventual outfalls of what we are doing to ourselves.

As you read this, you should realize that you are in the upper one-third quartile of our nation's total population who still reads to learn new things. Only those few of us who get beyond the television screen or the sports and comics sections of our daily newspapers are inclined to digest this type of material. You will find yourself comparing the content and my eventual premise to some of your own personal history, and your individual life style in our society's pecking order. You are also the type of person who senses that the world is not as it should be and are looking for some type of answer as to the cause.

I know, from my personal experience that in all communication it is imperative to understand where one is coming from in order to relate to the words being used. If not, there is so much room for misinterpretation leading into misdirection and wasted time. I also realize that you may differ in your perceptions of my views, which is my challenge to hopefully alter. So keeping this in mind, I will try to take this most convoluted and recklessly intertwined generation of ours and make some sense with you.

I am thankful for the use of this computerized world and the existence of the Internet, which generated many of the facts and figures that I'll be using in this dialogue. I am thankful too for the time that I have been provided to share these complex thoughts. I admire the good and even great writers who with pad and lead placed their thoughts on paper conditioned to think in a more organized manner, learning discipline of verse, able to influence the thoughts of others. I am far from these masters, so I will thank you beforehand for putting up with these awkward renditions and my grammatical mistakes that have been generated on the following pages.

I will keep this brief and hopefully informative, to hold your interest to the end and not turn you off, or away. I, like a growing number of us, am spiritually and personally concerned about the future world we are leaving to our children. I trust that you will accept that I am but a single messenger, just one of many today.

CHAPTER I
CONCEPTUAL THOUGHT

Each of us, at one time or another, has stared into the wondrous expanse of the universe and become humbled by its organization and largeness. We have wonderful working bodies and minds to feed our imaginations and an exceptional planet to support our life's travels. We live in a nation blessed with abundance and a government founded on freedoms unparalleled throughout all of recorded history. We are the result of all of our past human efforts and God's intervention, interacting with all life forms originally intended to feed off the other, for all of eternity.

When we reflect upon His, not our, world, we can feel a harmony, beauty, and balance within all living things. The drop of a leaf during the autumn season or a snowflake slowing and striking that same ground a few short months later, intuitively etches the heart and soul of each one of us into sensing something larger than ourselves. It is a visual, yet internal effect similar to a baby's smile and hug in its simplicity and understanding--and it's human warmth.

God has a unique way of talking to each one of us through our hearts and minds, and the intuitions of our souls. Through these soft, near silent messages, He is continually guiding us, throughout our entire lifetimes. Sometimes it is through the touch of another person who loves us very much; or a beautiful sunrise and sunset opening and ending a day, and other times, books such as this. And then there are moments of disastrous events that enter our conscious minds like the screams of a concerned parent sensing serious danger for His offspring. If we take time to listen to our surroundings, His messages lately, including the horrendous morning of 911, are like our natural parents sensing a major collision course. As we are an easily distracted population that needs to be clobbered between the eyes to become consciously aware, we are being inundated with consecutive sledgehammers through all of the events now taking place.

Today our world neighbors and Mother Nature with all of her energies are striking back at us with a fretful vengeance, trying to shake us from our current morass and personalized slumber. Perhaps through this, we can interpret that our latest tragedies of domestic terrorism, pestilence, fire, drought, flooding and our widening religious divisions as our personal hammers to wake up and start listening to the voice of this much larger world.

We are now finding that we are mutually coexisting in a global spaceship, filling with increasing numbers of human beings who also have their own personal demands for what the Earth and our collective psyches are no longer capable of digesting. In this, as all things have a "cause and effect", we are now losing the larger integrity of this world and the true potentials for our existence. It seems that we have been asleep at the wheel for a very long time, not wanting to be held accountable for what we have allowed to be transferred over these many years.

Today we are bombarded with increasing levels of disinformation and images showing us massive human carnage, corporate corruptions and political graft; that our oceans, fish, fowl and forests, and we in turn, are prematurely dying, with few of us thinking out the long-term ramifications of what we are becoming. These graphics are acting as an external message, trying to tell us that if we do not change what we are doing dramatically, we will be in deep trouble. All of this together is acting like the caged canary in a coal mine about to explode, loudly squawking a serious warning of an impending disaster.

Because of our present purchased values and personal distractions, our growing social and moral disasters were inadvertently caused in our chase to capture the brass ring. A ring better known as "The All American Dream." In this transition, from World War II to our modern times, we lost our moral compass as a nation, misdirecting our personal spiritual depth; not appreciating the larger responsibilities to what human life means.

This "stuff" was gradually infused into our lives in this race, as we were dealing with the struggles of just trying to survive the pressures of each day. In this, we unintentionally lost our generational focus and internal awareness, allowing our past universal freedoms to be assimilated into our present commercial and emotional bondage and this current world we are experiencing.

In our efforts to stay ahead of our times we gave little thought to the eventual development of human despair driven by anger, ignorance, frustration and human hate. We of this world are now sharing a life treadmill that is speeding around faster and faster, beyond anyone's ability to anticipate where we are going as a human society.

Because we consistently and emotionally treat the symptoms of things, we are now experiencing a physical probing to realize that we have placed too many artificial things including money ahead of God. We, as Americans, are very good at reacting against major calamities with a "crises management mentality" in the short-term, using money and physical force, then blaming Him when we fail. But we are very weak as a human body because we do not take the time to understand the origination of the conflict and its history; or think out the long-term repercussions of what we are doing to ourselves and in turn, to the rest of the World.

In this, our times have now converted into an era of the dangerous diversions of terrorism and the growing distractive shallowness of commercialism. All of the problems we share in our homes and in our personal lives and most of the corruptions around the globe are the result of us being out of sequence with our Father's reality and purpose.

If we are inclined to listen to the events of our times, there is a growing intuitive sadness being spoken within the bodies of our souls. A growing number of people are seeking something more meaningful for their lives, with spiritual depth and understanding. In this they are consciously seeking a deeper sense of purpose for their existence; hoping to move beyond our manufactured "feel-good at any cost" Westernized mentality of use, abuse and discard. They are finally realizing that we were not placed on this earth to just shop at our local malls.

Today, because of this reawakening, there is an escalation in global human prayer asking for God's intervention, to wave His magic wand making our problems disappear. A growing number pray that through His love the severe problems of the world will somehow be reversed. We are now, through the activities of our times receiving His response. We are being consciously awakened to the severity of our escalating damage, becoming attuned to the inner understanding that we are duplicating some type of past history. A history of so many other advanced civilizations being destroyed from within.

To counter our self-imposed and destructive natures, in God's loving way and man being who he is, we may someday conclude that all of us possess the ability to develop new avenues, re-engineering who and where we are.

History has shown, in brief spurts, that when people listen within themselves, then to do something positive with what is being heard, that man can positively reroute mankind's future evolution.

We, like all of our ancestors past, are again being given a multitude of conscious choices by these times; to hopefully address our many problems with what we sense, feel and intuitively believe, to revise this path we are on. Each of us can evolve in this awareness and understand that big pictures are made up of a lot of little pieces, and are all interrelated as patches of cloth in a mosaic woven by God.

We possess an intuitive sub-consciousness of knowing right from wrong, usually making the correct decisions when we take the time to listen within ourselves. All of us have this inborn ability to grow in a transitional faith while including each of our generations to develop the long-term answers. We should anticipate that the reality that our future generations will be inheriting what we envision from this moment on, and that each fragile day is but a gift.

A possible catalyst would be the retelling of our generation's story, which we initiated as children in a different and hopefully cleaner, format. By "reliving" this recent history, we can realize that what we accept for today's truth is slanted by other's interpretations, and that we are ignoring what we inherently sense. A story that we think we know so well, you will find has created our current misaligned priorities, distorting God's original intentions for all of us … His current disruptive and undisciplined children.

The retelling of our recent history not to just find fault and finger point, which is very easy to do, but to suggest a possible re-engineering of what and how we do things — to have us wake up as a free society. To not lose what is working well, but to improve upon what we have become. Perhaps we together can through this regenerate into our and His, original purpose, with a major concern about the eventual world all of us will be leaving someday, perhaps too soon.

CHAPTER II
EVOLUTION

As a child I thought that the world was going to be okay; that our generation would benefit from the sacrifices made by so many others who preceded our births. The *Leave it to Beaver's* and *I Love Lucy's* were and still are reflective of the innocence of the period. The white frame house surrounded by a freshly painted picket fence, with an oak, elm, and sycamore spreading their magnificence.

Mom was in the kitchen baking cookies with a glass of milk on the table waiting for us when we got home from school. Dad went to work at 7:45 in the morning and returned with a regularity of 5:30 each day. Dinner was served at 6:00 sharp. We were captured in this innocence, somehow believing that we would eventually build and leave a better world because of our intelligence and human ingenuity.

I, like many of you, lived an early existence where there was a semblance of sense and sanity in our society, an era of simplicity reflecting upon the innocence of the period. I retain childhood memories of the ambiance of living in a small community with pristine lakes and water that was drinkable. I remember, through a child's eyes and developing mind, the rolling hills near my early home. My inner sanctum in childlike wonderment was a self-entertaining environment driven by my imagination.

I recall the introduction of an early spring marked with regularity, a 2 p.m. local rainstorm, followed at 3:45 by a spectacular ending. The emergence of sunshine followed by a rainbow; the day's dirt washed away. I would ride the miniature water rapids contained by the ditch in the front yard of my home upon my return from school. The vehicle of choice was a 5-gallon washtub propelled by a broomstick and me hanging on for dear life. I don't remember the doctor pulling me out of the black hole of inner space during my birth, but I have a subconscious recollection of taking pride when I was land-bound crashing my bike against immovable objects to see if I could get them to move.

My early life was difficult and combative as all childhoods sometimes are, but not as hard as most, supported by love and the concern of my parents. I was spanked several times and missed a few dinner meals because I didn't listen at times, but out of this I learned right from wrong. I think back at this period with a reverence of the lessons learned, realizing now how I dropped the ball as a sire to my offspring.

I now know that life and what a parent gives to a child, oftentimes out of a loving concern, teaches us empathy and a sensitive understanding of our surroundings. And oppositely, if the parenting responsibilities are ignored, there is a heavy human emotional price to be paid by our following generations. I am finally realizing after five decades of life that my parents cared about what I would evolve into. A nurturing process similar, but on a much larger scale, to what our Father does for us, His creative, but easily disruptive children.

I remember what motivated me to do some of the things that I did, or didn't want to do, as a child. My allowance at that time was 25 cents a week for doing my household chores, which was a small fortune to me, and pretty much in alignment with the times. I could go to the movies on a Saturday morning for 15 cents. A soda and a box of popcorn would be added with the balance, allowing my friends and me to spend the better part of the day being entertained, a tradeoff for the labor of the week. I now look at what the average family of four spends to attend a ballgame or entertainment park and realize how much we have cost our children over these past decades.

When the collective "we" senses nothing unusual regarding a ballplayer or an actor, or a CEO who will earn more in one week than an average person will earn in his lifetime, I recognize that so many things that I accepted as normal are now far out of proportion. This is part of the catalyst, which prompted me to write these thoughts. That, along with this little inner voice which is now reawakening me spiritually, triggered by the events of that morning, September 11, 2001. And, my growing awareness of the future legacy I am leaving to my great-grandchildren.

I was told that I was so anxious to come into the world, that I did not have the patience to wait for the delivery room. I exploded into human life within the first 9 minutes of my mother's first labor pains. Her extreme discomfort,

I now personally realize, shared a large part of my DNA foundations of who, and what I would become as an adult in today's modern age.

It is said that 1,000 people can look at the same picture and when asked of their interpretations, one would receive 1,000 different answers to the same question. The human mind and the Earth's many languages, including English, do not provide an exacting science of a speakers, artist's or writer's intent. Our conscious emotional minds absorb so many of the same things differently, that the many complex issues in our lives have now become clouded, the depth and seriousness of our universal problems not consciously understood.

For well over three decades, I have been approached by my inner conscious to address the cause of my personal problems with some type of positive response. Over these years, I kept on doing what I was doing, placing myself in a consistent and deepening hole, losing out on so many of the opportunities that have been presented to my door. These years were filled with many personal frustrations in fits and starts, caused, as I now realize, by my personal resistance ... ignoring what was being said inside my soul.

It is only now, with my age advancing and with the loss of so many friends and family members for various health reasons, old age, stress and cancer etc., that I am finally trying to emotionally and spiritually sort all of this out. With God's patience with me, allowing for my free will and my personal mistake making, He has permitted many personal side trips to materialize; allowing me to recognize the results of many disastrous errors thereby bringing me back to where I should be, addressing the many larger causes.

I know that many of the Earth's past great civilizations got to a certain point in the evolutionary scale, then some outside force happened to them and they imploded. The Phoenicians, Greeks, Romans, the Mayans, and all other great societies were leaders in their day. Their presence, philosophies and politics influenced not only their immediate populations but also, eventually, the thinking of most of the Western World. The Phoenicians, Greeks, and Romans created the early paths for our monetary systems, industry, current moral thinking, and Westernized politics. The Mayan laid out an early, but detailed, forms of astrology, math, agriculture and medical surgical tools. I can believe that a certain part of their populations sensed that something was going wrong, long before their unseen downfalls.

I do not want to come across as a "Chicken Little" with a "the sky is falling" mentality. I believe that all things in history have their time and place and that those things, in their own way, will sort themselves out. But I know that I also have this gnawing feeling that things, although seeming normal, are not normal at all. That we are mirroring on a much larger scale the same path of wrong decisions made by our predecessors, well spelled out in our Christian Bible.

I now sense, along with a growing number of others that the initial terrorist attack on September 11, was another personal message to us to wake up as a nation and get our act together. To take in the reins on our growing responsibilities as a world leader and to finally let our real truth surface with the understanding that we are not invincible, before we lose what we have. And to learn that using politics or our military force in retaliation to anything is not the responsible answer to any of our growing societal problems on a global scale.

Instead of a more peaceful world being birthed because of our nation's existence, we are currently experiencing over 127 regional wars worldwide according to current U.N. numbers and an involuntary downsizing of Middle America, jeopardizing our future generations. Our political leadership is now talking "first strike" nuclear capacity to offset their inadequacies in negotiating our historical differences with others, rather than facing the much harder path of developing a compassionate human understanding for living in peace with each other.

I want you to realize that I am not a "doom and gloom" type of person; nor am I a proponent of the ultimate Armageddon prophesied in the Book of Revelations, realizing that if and when it happens, it is in God's hands. I simply appreciate my life and knowledge, and the undeserved blessings I hold.

I am thankful for waking each morning, healthy and living in the United States, having freedoms unsurpassed by any of our predecessors. I will, more often than not, take the time to check out the sunrises and sunsets each day, weather permitting, and on occasion smell the fresh air of each moment. In this reflection, I also find that I am in the throes of realizing each day produces a growing restlessness and lack of ease. The awkward world I knew as a child has now been replaced by a dangerous, foreboding existence I no longer know. Few of us have been prepared to understand this much larger picture of why our lives are becoming so difficult and so easily disposable.

Our current events are in the process of informing us that no matter who we are, or how much we have, or think we possess, that no one is immune from the dangers of these times. Today, our political and personal decisions, under the guise of progress and our national interests, are not permitting us the time to think things through before we do them anyway. We, and our current events are now homogenized in this process, with the vast majority of us being cloned to a sameness of mediocrity. We are becoming highly distracted by the minute and the manipulation of disinformation, separating us from our larger intuitive selves.

Because of my personal growing concerns for my grandchildren and their future offspring, I now place this at your doorstep for your eventual consideration, hopefully to have you listen from within, developing your own form of truth. I trust that somehow through this discourse, I will reach some part your conscious mind and heart to rethink where we are, and why we have so many unintended disasters as a free society under our God. Perhaps to have you and me and everyone else grow a little spiritually — and intellectually stave off some of our nation's arrogance and our personal self-abuse. Then through this, to create some new thought that will open a personal discussion between us that will have the real potential to lead us into a national alteration eventually affecting the balance of the world.

As you may already suspect, this book will have spiritual and religious overtones, including the use of many of our past secular decisions, which have led us to where we are today. I am not an overly religious person and am personally turned off by others who preach a hard line on the absolutes of Heaven and Hell, but I respect them for their views.

To clarify my position, I want you to know that I believe Jesus Christ is the greatest teacher and prophet of all time, and that all of the religions of the world have much to learn from His presence and teachings. His commitments and spiritual leanings were and are provided to lead us through our personal trials and global human divisions.

I believe that Jesus was placed on this Earth to educate all of God's grace and intent, to reach all cultures of mankind to overcome our humanly devised differences. It seems that when He was born all past historical recordings ceased being important. That our modern-day history began with His birth creating a new chapter for our personal and spiritual evolution.

He presented miracles establishing hope with simple explanations of who and what we could become as the children of our Father who created all. But with our human tendencies to make simple things complex and not listening well, instead of our growing together in peace and compassion with His existence we created our many current religious divisions. A modern-day filled with our growing human separateness—oftentimes it seems, with we at each other's throats.

I also believe that each one of us has the same capabilities of all of the spiritual masters since our beginning, including Christ, as we are all created in God's loving kindness with the ability of returning His unconditional love. Out of this, I am starting to believe that organized religion has unintentionally become a major problem because of human intervention.

I want you to know that the intent of this book is not to separate and divide or incur argument, but to eventually have each one of us realize that all of us on this Earth are unconditionally and equally loved by our Father. When you look at each of us around the world, you will find that we are all very much the same with similar wants and needs and personal desires, and most worship our only one shared God. Each of us inherently needs a moral and spiritual compass to be productive, earning a livable wage and protection from outside destructive forces. We want to believe that we are secure and will be appreciated for a life well lived from our work and activity, respected for our personal actions and who we are, and have hope for our tomorrows.

I recognize that outside the spiritual realm, each of us is a composite of all the genes we inherit from our parents and all of their parents before them, and are a product of our life experiences, both good and bad. All are either broadened or limited by the quality of our education, and the depth of the teachers and mentors we are exposed to during each stage in our lives. I also believe that these conditioning factors and each of the events and persons that happen in our secular lives have a meaning and sense of purpose. Each and all of the above intertwined to reach our subconscious minds, keeping us on track and focused spiritually.

It is for all of these reasons, and more, that I will use the following chapters and events as a point of reference to hopefully bring us together — to address the "cause and effect" of our secular divisions, with some plausible corrections utilizing our intuitive "free wills" and long dormant common sense. The Earth and our current manipulations, under the guise of human progress and governing, are now approaching a point of non-retrieval, in the real processes of destroying us from within.

CHAPTER III
GENERATIONAL CONDITIONING

As you can guess by now, I am a product of the ending of the Second World War. It was the start of a new generation where we idealistically believed that peace, prosperity and human compassion were to be driving forces of America. As children we were educated to embrace the notion that we were a nation managed under God to provide a beacon of trust and compassion, to aid the populations of this Earth. Through this, we were conditioned to believe that we were creating a positive future for many generations to come, just as our parents had. Perhaps to not struggle as hard, but to formulate a much better world because of our assets and ingrained intelligence creating a universal thought for hope.

At the time we intuitively believed, as children and young adults do, that we would create a better tomorrow learning from the human errors that led into the World Wars with their produced carnage and wasted costs. With this innocence, we wanted to eliminate the need for human strife and build a safer world through our educationally transposed ideals, intellect, and business enterprise. But instead of this happening, these idealistic goals and our virginity were lost to our nation's skewed, myopic priorities and our naivety over these past 50 years.

We presently reside in a country that has evolved into a puberty stage, becoming the most destructive nation on this world of God's we are trying to influence and protect. With less than six percent of the world's population, we consume and waste over 37% of the Earth's global productivity annually. An unintended arrogance developed in this transition, which has separated us from most others. The Second and Thirds Worlds are now trying to survive our nation's political decisions and consumptive habits, having to do without.

The human and ecological costs in our chase for what we believe to be essentials above all else, have now resulted in a form of randomness, a patchwork quilt creating our domestic human disharmony and a harbinger of increasing difficulty ahead.

It is said that our early lives lay the foundations of who and what we will be as adults, that the trials and tribulations experienced during our childhood establish our attitudes, perceptions and, ultimately, our beliefs, as we grow older. This process eventually evolves into our perceptions of what we will accept as the truth. If we place this on global terms, each nation duplicates these same transitions and errors of a human's maturation process of growing into a responsible adult. Every country goes through a birthing and maturing process eventually growing into a productive society; or, if conditioned by negative events becomes a belligerent, insecure and destructive adversary to their world neighbors.

Today a person living in the slums of the world or on the streets of America has a similar set of priorities as the successful individual running corporate America. And a person living in poverty, born in the Second and Third Worlds and indoctrinated to hate, is going to someday have that conditioning surface. A lifetime of negative secular conditioning, on all levels and all fronts, which is what we are now currently experiencing domestically, providing us with the potential view of what our children will eventually endure.

Our parents' generation had the same innate hope as children of creating a better tomorrow for themselves, building on what they inherited. They experienced the trying times of surviving the Great Depression and living the World Wars, and were the great part of building Middle America. These people lived a life of having to do without, sacrificing what little they had, doing the best they could during those trying periods with answers. They also wanted a better and easier world for their children because of their love and past hardships. They held the intuitive, unspoken belief that we, their children, would in turn improve upon what they had initiated.

I now appreciate the many sacrifices my parents and their generation made, and the obstacles they had to overcome through their efforts of hard labor and ingenuity. With a higher level of awareness that comes with age, I can now look into the eyes of this generation and see the effects of these many years. The lines etched into their skins reflect the decisions they've made and the individual lives they lived. The eyes of some are bright and sparkling, inquisitive and smiling, full of life, still possessing a sense of humor, handling each day with thankfulness as it comes. And the others, a growing balance of this number, are tremendously sad, empty, and disappointed. Many fearing a perceived absolute of death, their lives dramatically unfulfilled. I also see, out of all of this, the balance and wonderment of the many new lives being born. A renewed energy which our God generates, with new souls inhabiting their little human bodies with so much potential, replacing that which is being lost.

God and human life offers so many continual opportunities that it is most difficult to know what is right most of the time. We too often allow our emotions to block our common sense thinking, making the wrong choices too often. The time spent from our childhoods to becoming productive adults, understanding this correlation is something we have been ill educated to understand and personally use to our universal advantage.

It has been said that it takes almost five decades of living life to get a vague understanding of what is going on and then spending the rest of one's life trying to sort out this knowledge. With the benefit of this insight we can realize that over our years random events, some natural and others more numerous man-made, have transformed all of us through these experiences we call societal progress. With all of the inroads made, we have been acclimated by our actions to bury our heads in the sand, conditioned to ignore our harsh larger realities as a human society.

The scientific and technological advances of our times have presented to a small minority of us temporary luxuries and bouts of prosperity, but at a high cost to our children's generation and the rest of the world. In this transference we placed our future destiny into the secular hands of our lawyers, politicians, and corporate America; disregarding the fact that we have entered an era that is overwhelming our intuitive inner psyches.

We now find ourselves inundated with all the negatives in our lives, not able to access the cause of our difficulties, not able to look at our misperceptions and ourselves as the real problem. Today, because of the lack of using common sense, politically, we elect to repair the damage of a riot or financial failure rather than invest or regulate these arenas before they are burned or bankrupted. The trillions of tax dollars spent to reconstruct, or create bailouts for human mismanagement, could have financed the refurbishing of our educational systems and our inner cities and the rest of this world. Training programs could have been created through the use of the private non-profit sectors developing cottage industries addressing our many identified social ills, not only here in the United States, but also worldwide.

In hindsight, this could have initiated new employment and individual self-worth with long-term vision and a more eco-balanced world. New jobs and methods of training could have been implemented globally, building individual self-esteem in joint-business ventured enterprises which could have perhaps staved off the mentality that struck us that September morning. Instead, we have over 90% of all of the world's lawyers practicing law in this country, myopically arbitrating our deadly habits of human conflict. Because of our societal priorities based upon money and mismanaged by the lack of long-term vision, we do not know how to peaceably talk with each other and concentrate for any length of time ... the root cause of our many legal problems.

This modern day evolution is leaving many of us spiritually empty, longing for direction and seeking some form of emotional relief. All of the secular problems we have in our lives and the national tragedies we mutually experience are the result of our actions of all generations past and present. Over 96% of us recently polled in the Christian world say we believe that there is a God, but if we truly accepted His existence and His love, we would not be experiencing the many problems that we have in this secular world of ours.

From the days of our Nation's founders we have been the clients involved in the short-term decisions of too many influential people with shortsighted agendas, contrived for political and monetary gain, power, and prestige. To address the problems and opportunities of our future we will have to consider where our government is in our lives and what we can expect from its future actions. Then open ourselves to become fully responsible for all others and our God who created all. Using what precious time each of us has left and this method of understanding we can also identify the true purpose for our lives living on this planet, Earth.

Today we are being challenged, as each generation is challenged, to get into the basics of living our lives with some common sense values, moving into a more aware level of thinking. By using our intuitions and allowing God's presence to surface, we can use all of our successes and past failures to alter our thinking. In doing this we can learn from our short history and the decisions of others who have gone through the trials and errors of their human existence.

If we are still listening to the messages of the 11th, we can recognize that each of us is being personally challenged to grow beyond the massive death and evil of others in remembrance of the lives lost. That day, and all of its following events were provided to us as a consistent reminder that we are currently the receivers of what we have done to this planet Earth. Because of this, we are now being asked by all of the events of our times to awaken from our slumber, with an understanding of the much larger and kinder picture our Creator represents.

We have many serious and complex problems in this country and world of ours, well documented and reported. Our human and ecological devastations are so massive and potentially deadly in scope that they will need to be addressed by some very serious people with a major sense of urgency. If we fail to evolve in this thinking, there is a growing chance that the world we had, as children, will be lost forever, as we, ourselves, have created all of our dysfunctions and misery on this planet that some think is ours.

So much has been written and said about the incompetence and the disruptive nature of our life styles, the corruptions of money, power, religion, and our politics ... that I am hesitant to duplicate these words, but these words and thoughts are necessary to have us understand what has happened to our generational ideals. For this reason, I want to inform you that some of what you will read will be in perhaps too much detail and depth in text form, getting away from what I had hoped, twenty-six years ago, to keep in light, generalized and maybe humorous terms. I am now listening to my intuitions, trying to do what I am intuitively being told. I know from personal experience that God has a tendency to use and guide us, when we are open to His direction.

The following are but a few examples of our "cause and effect" and some suggestions to create some verbal discourse between our Father and us; to perhaps create something good with our lives, while we are still here. I do not pretend to have any of the answers and would hold any who think they do as irresponsible and arrogant. I hold no degrees or personal experience in massively changing this world. I am like you and everyone else, just getting by with the challenges and struggles in my life, now listening to the messages within my soul. And hoping that I am making more right decisions than wrong, surviving the pressures and my growing concerns of these times.

As any creative baker will say, it's not just the ingredients you place together, but also the time, experience and personal care that creates a great cake. How we get out of these times, creating a better world for our children, will take more than a little flour and water and a much larger appreciation of the world we have just made. With that said, we will begin this journey, so kick back, please open your mind and have patience with me.

CHAPTER IV
DYSFUNCTIONS

It has been said many times, that we Americans need to experience a major catastrophe before we notice a problem. Until then, we have a tendency to bury our heads in the sand, the ostrich effect, hoping our problems will fix themselves with little discomfort. It is also said that when a society does not pay attention to its politics that history will repeat it-self. Our recorded past has shown that when this happens, a handful of privileged insiders will take advantage of the ignorance, the emotions and the eventual apathy of the general public.

Today with so much bad news surrounding us, we hope that, in one way or another, some common sense thinking will someday prevail to address our many growing human pressures. In this, we would like to believe that our current discomfort be addressed by some sound minds that will create a better lifetime. We don't really know how this is going happen, but we trudge along, hoping for the best, trusting our Nation's leadership to come up with our answers. You and me, being among the enlightened bunch also know that our government, or any government, is not structured to be all knowing and benevolent in its social actions.

It would be political suicide to discuss the events of our times with raw, possibly distasteful long-term resolutions to address the many real problems we have. That party would be drummed out as not being credible; the media would have a field day. For those in power there would be too much to lose. And yet this is what this book is about. We Americans have pursued the innate artificial dream of having it all. We don't want to hear that we are in the process of now losing it all.

Sometimes we think that we are protecting what we have, yet we are experiencing a governing system that is in the process of discovering that it is ill equipped to accommodate our personal parenting for us. Each day our headlines are filled with news of our horrendous events that are crying out for visionary and benevolent governing and regulation ... and it's not there. Negative news, that used to rarely be in our headlines thirty years ago, is now a daily, growing occurrence. Our corporate financial scandals, stock market manipulations, past savings and loan institutions financial bailouts, our impending social security systems failures, and our high health and future social indebtedness are but a few current examples of our ineptness in addressing the problems of this nation and world, politically.

Since the mid-1960s, while our gross domestic product tripled, supposedly improving our lives, violent crime increased almost 600%. Divorces have doubled, the percentage of single parent homes has quadrupled and more than 70% of our minority births occur out of wedlock. We lead the world in murder, rape and violent crime, and environmental damage because of our widening socioeconomic divisions. These many events are the result of our now developed commonality of apathy and personal distractions of just trying to survive over these past 50 years.

Instead of a better world being created because of our generational talent and "supposed" intelligence, we relinquished our democratic roles in living in a free society to a small handful of political insiders. A small conditioned segment of our world's population, who know how to manipulate the system of private and public enterprise, who now dominate the decisions of corporate and political America.

These executives and politicians are trained through the trials and errors of competitive battle to seek shortcuts, to generate as much control and profit in the short-term, at the long-term expense to our country and the world at large. Today, our political system is a methodology in which money, power and profit feed on themselves, unintentionally but directly corrupting the players, historically leading into a disastrous disadvantages for the public and now threatening our Nation's democracy.

When we were young adults, the United States provided hope for the rest of the world. We were perceived to be a bastion of strength and corporate morality, based on unparalleled freedom of thought and action. When our religious institutions and "we", permitted Congress to become our self-appointed surrogate parent through our nation's "Great Society Programs", we stepped back from our responsibilities to each other as human beings, especially in the terms of parenting our children.

Under the guise of creating a better world for all, we inadvertently allowed our government to intrude in social and capitalistic areas never outlined, or incorporated, in our Constitution, or in our human spirits. It is a digression, which if we take time to digest these intrusions created the secular foundations of our inefficient political and corrupt corporate systems. It also in this transference molded our current perceptions.

We know that the very nature of surviving the electoral methods we presently use distorts the thoughts of the well intentioned, favoring just a handful of people. Each community has stories filled with immoral, unethical behavior with political decisions that fly in the face of using common sense for the good of all. Each compromise, though it may be small at the time, squeezes a little more lifeblood out of what this community and the Earth can physically and morally support. City and county governments pass approvals over common-law and past experience of disastrous proportions, with a handshake and a wink to political insiders.

For the few dollars invested by those with deep pockets, political decisions are swayed for personal gain to a small handful of people. Compromises are made, short-cutting the intentions of a democracy, selling the integrity of the human soul for a few pieces of silver. It may be to a lawyer or a local land developer who wants to squeeze one more home into a comprehensive development plan already approved to protect the ecology and the local infrastructure; or it may be a rider tacked onto a Congressional bill to secure federal tax benefits and bond monies to build a sports or business complex to profit the insiders exorbitantly.

Unromantic as it may seem businesses are created to make money and profit. Business plans to have this happen are arranged either formally on paper, or in one's head. If management makes more right choices than wrong, the company prospers and grows. The process is similar to a child's nurturing properties from birth to a productive adulthood, mirroring the stages of crawling, to walking and then the running stages of adult maturity.

Since it is human nature to sometimes shortcut the outcomes of our decisions and effort (to produce a result as quickly as possible), strategic planning analyzes the many parts of the whole to accelerate these steps to the advantage of a paying client. This process identifies any possible outside pressures and market forces and anticipates, then molds, through manipulation, a future outcome. As competitive pressures grow in the business world, as all things have a cause and effect, upper management is forced to re-engineer their internal operations, or else merge and acquire to survive.

If this path is selected, management will seek a synergistic or strategic fit through a friendly or hostile takeover, and approach Wall Street or other funding resources to capitalize in their "wants and needs," which personally benefit the insiders. If they are unsuccessful in this endeavor, the company will lose market share and be forced to downsize; or be absorbed by a competitor. If this avenue fails, the company will then file for bankruptcy, to the loss of its employees and stock investors.

A very small handful of these business professionals, who are successful in this aggressive, battle-hardened world, become extremely wealthy with insider manipulation and are honed by these personal strategies and wars for survival to seek additional advantages. Over time, the many ideals of their youthful innocence are eventually chipped away, at the disastrous expense of this nation's corporate moral and ethical fiber. This leads into creative bookkeeping practices, AKA "cooking the books" for income reporting and tax evasion, stock manipulations, IPO's for immediate wealth creation, and the persuasion of favorable political decisions.

Our government has the sole responsibility of protecting its' citizens from outside invasion while maintaining law and order, protecting those who have from the intrusions of others. The governing process is supported through a tax system for operating revenue to cover its' overhead expenses. When a large company or it's industries strategic plan anticipates a change in the tax law or additional government spending, the marketing and financing programs incorporate the efforts of lobbyists to act as their sales agents protecting their turf and self interests. Out of this, we have existing "good old boy" committee networking and "pork barrel" programs being manipulated by partisans that demand spending trillions and borrowing billions of dollars each year, with financial underwriting efforts far removed from the intentions of our nation's founders.

Most persons outside this stratum of corporate and political manipulation, who are not making enough to pay their bills, are being squeezed. They are the pawns that are coming to the conclusion that life on this Earth is very difficult and dangerous, and based on their personal conditions, are finding life a living hell.

Today, with few exceptions, we have evolved into a nation being led by persons who are financially and socially far removed from the rest of America, a socioeconomic group intent on keeping the power they purchased for profit, control and business reasons. The financial pressures on our middle class families, our retailers, and manufacturers, and the neighborhood store, are currently in a deadly serious game attempting to survive the decision making by the "haves" and the serious outfall it is causing. We now have evolved into being used in a political and global financial game where no one wins, except for this handful of people.

While political and democratic overhaul and possible downsizing of government operations is occasionally postured for appeasing the cry of the masses for re-election purposes, as things now stand, and human nature being what it is, this will never happen. Our worlds of psychology, sociology and money recognize that it is human nature to not be willing to give up what we believe is an earned entitlement and the possible loss of these "entitlements" are the fears that are played upon, maintaining a status quo mentality.

Capitalizing on this, our representatives, or those individuals running for political office or controlling corporate manipulations, are constantly forced to promise to correct our many real and perceived problems without going into the specifics of the why and how, knowing their eventual costs. Today, we support a political leadership trying to appease the financiers for their short-term support, who successfully convince us into believing that we are getting what we think we deserve.

It is not to the player's advantage to address these arenas for dramatic change, as the vast majority of us, and they, and our families, will be financially hurt in the process of any correction. For this reason, our fears and entitlements are constantly stroked, the voices of reason downplayed by a convoluted law-making process, with smoke screens devised, keeping us distracted by the minutiae in our lives. The end result is that each day we are saturated with never-ending news of the horrendous tragedy of conflict of man vs. man and nation vs. nation, and all in a wasteful confrontation against nature, our common sense, and God; not using our commonsense.

One would think that as educated as we think we are, that this situation would dictate that we take politics, greed and corruption out of our lives immediately, yet the vast majority of us are motivated to do things driven by emotion and money, conditioned to think for short-term results. We, bottom line, do not want to lose our present comfort zones and what stature we think we have, hoping against hope that God will somehow intervene to save us from loss of what we think we own.

The hurdle holding us back is that we have been sleeping at the wheel as a generation. We have allowed America to evolve into a country whose future is now being sold to the highest bidders and manipulators. An era of allowing the chief executive officers of corporate America and the world, who are under extreme pressure to report an increasing profit every quarter, to buy and control as much political influence as possible. Their motivation, like any of us, is to protect what they have personally accomplished through their expertise and effort, while maintaining and profiting from what they "think" they control.

Instead of being governed with benevolence, compassion and insight, we are reaping the results of the weaknesses of human nature and short-term greed. We have now been fragmented into conflicting personal and financial divisions, instead of being a cohesive whole as a country. The result, when tied into our technological advances, has produced an unfocused population unable to cope with today's speeding and reckless society. A country led by others not willing or able to listen to the simple words originating from our mutual God to have us live in peace with each other.

Our domestic and foreign policy mirrors the past efforts and history of Rome, England, Spain and France, all leading up to the events of 911, but on a different global scale. We either attempt to control others by sponsoring dictatorships, buying local politics, or by manipulating the populations with handouts of humane programs and military and financial aid, with little filtering down to those actually in need. The bin Laden's, Hussein's, Noreiga's and Marco's of the world were, and are, products of our nation's intrusive failures of choosing the wrong sides of governing ideologies to support at the time.

On the opposite more personal side of this spectrum, we are now in the mode of being spiritually challenged to use our wisdom and intelligence collectively, placing God to the forefront of our thoughts before we act. We reside within one of the few working, yet extremely challenged, democracies in the world. We are blessed with natural resources, including a thinking work force and technology to move information and to educate. Most persons living in this country still want to be responsible for their actions and have hope for their futures. Despite all the internal challenges we have as a population, we selectively will, and instinctively do, help those in need anywhere on this earth.

We are still a benevolent people driven by the principles of developing moral decisions. We are also in an overt desperation, seeking a road map to eventually let us know where we are going and how we are going to get there. We are presently experiencing the result of our past political indifference, our ignorance of our larger human motivations and our personal non-involvement, allowing our government to devise our individual destinies without concern for the human spirit.

We have the potential of instituting massive compassionate change in developing this third chapter of ours, the first two being the agricultural and industrial ages of our nation's evolution. When we realize how we will be affected by thinking out our "cause and effect", combined with massive imaging of future possibilities, a new path can be created that will benefit all; moving us beyond our artificially induced confinements through this age of technology. In this, we can weigh the results of each past decision with practical well thought out solutions, but on humane and more personal terminologies for revision.

We now have the responsibility as God's children, while residing in a free nation, of leading not only ourselves, but also the rest of the world, into the 21st Century through our example and intellect. Our future opportunities will be derived through the recognition that it is our generational challenge to revise this path we are traveling with a clear understanding of where we are and why. With planned purpose and future focus, we can digest our various options and learn to work with each other with long-term vision and intellectual enterprise. We posses an infrastructure that, while showing surface fatigue, has the capability of reversing many of the breakdowns and social problems we presently share.

The internal messages we sometimes feel, contained in our hearts, minds and souls, will someday lead us to look at things in a different light. In this we are being challenged to listen to the simple dictates that come from within each of us and to grow this listening prowess. And to discern fact from fiction with the understanding that what has transpired over the past five decades has created what we are today. With these energies and the use of the media and the Internet, our suppressed truth will finally surface, providing an intensive era of enlightenment. Through this we can find that there is a positive universal harmony out there to benevolently guide us. We just have to devise the methods to use it to our advantage.

We have a growing segment of our population and leadership who recognize that things are not working right and there is a need for transitional repair, a segment that can be tapped into eventually. These numerous energies have initiated concepts that are, or have the potential of prudently working, if their voices can be heard above the obvious objections as we grow out of our reactive mode. The eventual outcome, when heard, can produce a national re-engineering of our government's activity and our personal social programming.

The God within us is asking us to get our house back in order, allowing our free will to surface using our intuitive awareness and His direction; to have each one of us start thinking on a higher plane of reference as to who we are and what we have become as His children. Each of us can come to the realization that we are now in the process of developing a future in spite of ourselves. We can do it stupidly by thinking in the emotional short-term, not taking from the message of that September morning. Or we can intelligently plan for our mutual tomorrows. Our future like all futures past is going to happen either way.

It was Karl Marx who originated the philosophical thinking that organized religion is the opiate of the masses. This thinking led into the later cult mentality of Hitler's "give me a child before he is seven years of age, and I will emotionally and mentally control that person for the rest of his lifetime." This is the same underlying premise and conditioning that our "Capitalistic Democracy", by encouraging our chase for the "All American Dream" also captivated our adult mindsets today living in America.

What we do from this day forward, and how we do it now, will have the same affect on our succeeding generations as ours is doing with us. God did not intend us to be robots, but gave us the free will to be imaginative in what we do, think and say, which makes this a very interesting period. It is because of this, that the balance of this book is but a first small step to have each one of us reach into our memory banks and listen to our hearts, understanding some of our recent events, and their ramifications.

CHAPTER V
CAUSE AND EFFECT

Our many world critics believe that we are growing fat and corrupt, losing our moral compass and direction. There is a growing perception that we are experiencing similar events that destroyed our predecessors from within. It has also been shown to these same people, that when we make up our minds to accomplish something, we either get involved in developing the solutions or run over those who are the problem.

I have a professional background in business management and consulting to include mergers and acquisitions, on a nationwide basis. It is a professional world dealing with human shortsightedness, insecurities, incompetence, fear, and enormous greed. Inadvertently, many of the participants lose their spiritual focus, with one's more important lifetime priorities becoming skewed, chasing the deal. Since the morning of September 11, 2001 this industry, like many others has hemorrhaged to the point of hurting me financially. Through this my personal priorities and overviews have changed establishing a different path for my stability. By emotionally experiencing these multiple disasters, I am now becoming more spiritually focused and aware of my much larger purpose.

God continually talks to us individually and collectively through all that enters our lives for our lifetimes. This is something we sense intuitively as children, but seem to retire this capacity as we mature, perhaps growing jaundiced by dealing with our grown-up struggles of life. Today because of this, I have an evolved concern about the future type of world we are leaving to our children — not just our finances and the ecology, but every other area as well. I have come to believe that people and events, and the personal setbacks we experience come into our lives for a specific reason.

With this in mind, the larger events that led up to, and followed, the disaster of that morning brought many things back into a personal perspective for me. Because of this, I thoroughly believe that September 11 was another message, perhaps a slap in the face, to all of us in America to wake up to the larger responsibilities we have to our children's generation and to act on these responsibilities while we are still on this Earth.

God has His own way of specifically communicating with each one of us, trying to gain our conscious attention. It is through all of our life's circumstances and our decision-making that our Father allows us our freedom to grow spiritually, and to hopefully learn from our past errors in our maturing process. His unconditional love tries to keep us focused and centered, our souls grounded to His original intentions. It is through this vehicle that we are now receiving the results of the many decisions that our nation made during our lifetimes, an era now becoming accelerated by human shortsightedness and corporate greed.

Personally, I have found that our Father communicates and forgives through loving events, allowing us to heal, learn, and mature in a peaceful manner. All the good in the world, all the happenings we call miracles, are the result of His existence and His concern. And other times, when His message is ignored, He allows bad things to happen. This is part of our spiritual evolution, to mature from what is learned, to grow more dependent upon Him. He also occasionally allows us our "free will" decisions to hit ourselves between our eyes causing disappointment and pain, even to the point of His accepting human genocide, as we discovered on the 11th.

It is through these events that we gain strength and an intuitive insight through this process, overcoming pain and adversity, becoming loving and forgiving adults, listening to the message inside each of our souls. He does the same thing with a nation's development, good and bad, providing a lesson of trust and hope, yet leaves a secular light at the end of the tunnel for all of His children, and this Earth.

Today we are being forced to recognize that all of the ecological and human carnage and misery we are exposed to locally, nationally, and globally is self inflicted, and so unnecessary — and also to become aware that our experiment of governing by a democracy is currently jeopardized, with the true possibility of failing.

I now believe that our "feel good mentality", which ebbs and flows with our financial security and market performance, has created an atmosphere more dangerous than the period of the Cold War. During our lifetimes we became sheep in a flock, following a reckless path as a nation, insensitive to our much larger spiritual responsibilities to ourselves and, in turn, to this planet. We are living in a time that is now evolving into what we are today, a misguided and mis-prioritized nation that believes in our self-entitlements above all else, including God, while we unknowingly self-destruct.

The nature of this new millennium, with its first opening round, can be digested as being deadly serious and personally challenging, solely dependent on your perceptions of these times. For many observers, it seems as if we have now entered a period of a modern day *Twilight Zone* of unknown and perplexing origins.

Many of our hearts, minds, and souls were touched as they have never been touched before by the events of 911 and in a way that, to this time, will never be duplicated. We were caught with our pants down, losing our nation's virginity, personally and politically naive to the composite hatreds and destructive vent of other nations around the globe. We are now, as with all great nations of our past, on a threshold of becoming a nation maturing to another level, perhaps moving out of our teenage puberty.

We have a history of rising from the storms of impending doom and converting the moments into brilliant success. We lead the world in scientific advances, industrial productivity, and innovative thinking. We are the richest country in the world, not only in Gross National Product, but also in talent and arguably human and religious rights. Because of our religious foundations and our personal inventiveness, we are the freest and most compassionate country on this spaceship. Our divisions are made whole because of our human diversity and being blessed by God, and, as one, we bring hope to many others throughout the globe.

We provide thousands of tons of food and medicines to others around the Earth daily to address their needs and desperation. We explore the far heavens and the deep caverns of this Earth because of our wondering about why things are as they are, curious about their existence. We will, for obvious reasons, place our lives on the line to protect our standards of living and religious beliefs against evil oppression and human misery throughout the world. With all that has been said about our weaknesses, most persons would sacrifice all that they have to live here, warts and all.

We are a country made up of people from over 167 different nations, according to our latest census, separated by the personal misconceptions created by our upbringing, by our homes' locations, and by where we are in the commercial loop. We are what we are because of the genes we inherit from our parents and all of their parents before them, our formal and informal education, and the minds and experiences we were exposed to while we were maturing. Out of this, we formulate our habits and interpretations, taking from our life's experiences, which not only govern what we think is true, but also the responses we experience from others.

A business consultant is conditioned and educated to quick study "cause and effect" in order to implement solutions for future corporate change. I have taken this same premise in formatting *A Child's Legacy*, but explained in human terms, on a local and national, then global description scale. In this, the following words that you will read will outline our recent history that laid the foundations to what we are currently experiencing.

By applying an analyst's approach, I will dissect where we have been, where we are now and where have the potential to go. I will outline the results of many of our serious and growing problems, then explain its' history in some depth as to the origins. I ask you to understand that this writing is not to just find fault and leave it at that, but also to provide plausible alternatives that are visionary in their approach. The overall premise is not designed to focus on the negatives, but structured to have us become aware of our surroundings and eventually open a personal, then national discussion for compassionate, common sense civil change.

History has shown that it is the lack of any nation's long-term focus on human nature, foreign policy, and planning for one's domestic future, that creates crises management. Man is very good in absorbing this mentality, pulling the strings of cooperation with money and force, addressing human needs and atrocities around the world. We are very poor in anticipating and planning things out in a compassionate manner for long-term earthly support.

When we are inclined to think out the cause of certain things, we can conclude that a single person, not a group, always initiates atrocities and pain. Hitler was abused as a child, his father forced into bankruptcy by Jewish bankers who knew he could not pay. The simple love and supportive existence that he could have received in his early years instead evolved his thinking into revenge against an entire race to counter his childhood conditioning. Stalin of Russia, Hussein (who headed up the torture programs of Iraq before becoming president), Mao of China, and all the rest of this ilk fit this same psychological profile as they were physically abused, conditioned by poverty, and unloved by their natural parents; and were the recipients of severe hardships during their early lifetimes. Each became vengeful, caught up in a powerful and negative aspect of mind twisting events, each evolved into a disastrous response as adults.

All of them lost their childlike perspective of innocence while gaining power with little, if any, respect for human life. All, including bin Laden, who was born to wealth, experienced the downside of losing their civility and sense of purpose, corrupted by their egos and internal pain, and the broken promises of adults, allowing the dark side of the mind to prevail. Each found it necessary to gain power and then manipulate human fear, prestige, money and personal control to strike back at their perceived offenders as their own form of revenge.

All the human genocides, child and spouse abuse, World Wars, plagues, poverty and terrorism, including September 11, are the result of mankind not being educated to respect life and the loving balance provided by our mutual God. All of our social ills, our ecological damage, and financial problems are a result of not listening to that voice inside each one of us, ignoring the loving directions of our Creator. The message to be good stewards to ourselves, by using our natural giftedness in a benevolent manner and by supporting this world around us, is consistently ignored by us in an arrogant manner in our chase for wealth and personal security.

Instead of using our genius, talents, and prosperity to create a better world with vision, we destroy for immediate results, not wanting to understand the long-term cost and the eventual human ramifications. We build communities in areas that are prone to flooding, fire, sinkholes, and earthquake to profit the landholder, developer, insurer and bank. When some type of ecological damage affects that area with hurricane, erosion, or drought, we envelope the event as an "Act of God", not wanting to blame ourselves for building in areas never designed to support development. We come to the aid of others in this world in the short-term, not understanding their histories and culture, and then leave in a lurch; creating more problems than we solve.

We initially ignore the efficient use of our peacekeeping infrastructures, NATO and UNESCO of the United Nations, thinking we can perform better than they ever will. We back the Shah of Iran, Marcos of the Philippines, Hussein of Iraq, and the al Qaeda with weapons and military support, and then exit each country allowing evil, ignorance, and poverty to prevail. We leave a country that started an altercation to be governed by a person who was abused and unloved as a child. We create social and military programming and lawmaking in this process without examining the long-term potential of the damage being created for short-term political and monetary gain.

Today, we domestically build technologies and exploit management decisions to maximize profit on a quarterly basis, to build the balance of our financial portfolios as quickly as possible, not understanding the long-term consequences on the rest of the world and the resultant repercussions. The past rioting on our city streets and the individual positioning of special interest groups, the causes complex and narrowly viewed, are the result of the disrepair of our nation's priorities of placing the love of money return over the collective moral needs of ourselves.

Through our years, we have become conditioned to seek immediate gratification for what we do, not educated to realize the personal and psychological ramifications of what we have been doing to ourselves, corporately. Our unwillingness to intelligently invest in the educational needs of the general public to think in broader terms has produced the lack of common sense in ethically and prudently managing ourselves. It seems in this process that we have been conditioned, like a child in a toy store with his arms full, to want more, no matter the future cost.

The average American has been conditioned to care more about making money and having ice cubes in their freezer, protecting their jobs and lifestyles, than in understanding the responsibilities that come from living on this Earth governed by a democracy. Our educational systems instead of developing morally driven, ethical people (motivated by human compassion and sensitive, intuitive understanding of this physical blessing), produce individuals forced to make short-term decisions for immediate gratification. We are a nation that takes our best and brightest minds and alters the internal driving motivations we naturally have as children, to allow economics to take precedence over our childlike, common sense thinking.

We are now governed to produce the palm of the hand, extended horizontally, to receive what has been given too easily. When these monies and programs are not easily forthcoming, the hand turns into a vertical position of manipulating for financial gain, or holding a gun. Or, in a more obtuse and destructive manner, lobbying efforts initiated to underwrite new law- making to protect the wants and needs of corporate America. When one listens to the message of our current events, our minds, hearts and souls are silently screaming at us to start listening to what is going on around us.

Our times are challenging each one of us to become sensitively aware of how fragile and precarious life is, and to recognize the extent of the abuse we have inflicted on what we inherited so very long ago. We can grow personally and spiritually through the ruins of that September morning, taking from the loss of life and its message and turning it into something positive —

or we can keep on doing what we have been doing and experience the true potential of unintentionally creating a more foreboding world.

We, in this country, are now in the third evolutionary level of using our intuitive abilities to do something with what we inherently sense. To recognize that this fragile experiment of human life being governed by a democracy is now being challenged to move into a new era of political and personal direction, in need of a massive overhaul. For never in the times of all recorded history have we, as humankind, done so much damage to this planet and ourselves in such a short period of time.

Although no human mortal can project the eventual outcome of 911, it is safe to assume that we have entered an era of the biggest challenge of our generation. That what is personally decided in our hearts, souls, and minds in the near term will determine the direction of our country and our personal futures. We are now living in a period that is asking each of us to grow through our current events to personally think out where we are at this moment in time, to listen to the world around us, and to our inner selves. And to grow through this process of simply existing, and to recognize the spiritual responsibilities that each of us has to one another while living on this planet, Earth.

The opportunities of our following generations are to recognize that the vast amounts of our difficulties are self-induced and, hopefully, correctable given enough time, energy and talent; and that our current perceptions keep us divided. It is our spiritual and generational challenge to revise this journey we are naturally traveling, with a clear understanding of where we are and why; learning from our past mistakes and our personal desperations and then to do something positive with this experience and knowledge as quickly as humanly possible.

Each of us has the enormous untapped inner potential of instituting massive, compassionate change within ourselves, to think on global terms. To realize, that what we do individually and corporately in our hearts, minds, and souls, has a trickle up potential. To come to the realization that we have made our lives far more difficult than our Father ever intended. In this we can learn to understand the "cause and effect", then develop the wisdom to use this information wisely, in a compassionate personal manner. To introduce a massive human reawakening to start listening to the direction of our Father, and to learn to do things differently by listening to that inner voice that we call our subconscious and intuition. And to accept that our God is real for our use and not to be taken for granted.

By developing this concept through an opened mind, tied in with prayer and a business plan, we can refocus ourselves to eventually reprogram this country of ours. Then, through our personal experiences, this spiritual walk tied in with the many new lessons we will learn, to benevolently affect the thinking of the rest of the world. To allow our same God to provide us with the wisdom and knowledge, to have the disasters of Washington, D.C., Manhattan, N.Y., and a small agricultural field outside of Pittsburgh evolve into something positive; to tie-in our historical knowledge with the modern world, electronically collecting all that we have and confront the unknown. That two to three generations from now, all the world's children will have the similar chances and outlooks and dreams that we had when we were children simply growing up. We just need visionary leadership and the personal will with an opened heart, to get us there.

For whatever reason, not easily defined or expanded upon by our Western philosophies, our souls and our physical selves could be existing in a country that persecutes and slaughters its citizens. We could have been born in a Third World country or in the slums on the Earth, with desperation for survival increasing with each passing second. Instead, our physical presence is blessed with natural resources, living in a nation which still functions with a level of freedom; still dependent upon a thinking mind.

CHAPTER VI
FINANCIAL REALITY

According to the non-profit Washington tax-study group, Citizens for Tax Justice, our federal government will extract $3.4 trillion dollars from the domestic economy this year. Over one third of United States total gross production and business output is spent on social programs alone, not including our local cost of governing ourselves -- and the increasing financial obligations of our global war machines.

Today, fewer than 600 corporations dominate our economy and support political lobbyists who know how to control political compromise. Presently, one tenth of one percent of all domestic corporations own more than two thirds of all business holdings nationally. Sixteen of our largest companies with annual pretax incomes in the hundreds of billions of dollars paid no taxes last year, while receiving tens of billion dollars in government subsidies.

Our fifty largest banking conglomerates control 60% of all deposits globally, and the fifty largest companies have interlocking directors on the boards of these corporations. Their decisions then respond to the expectations of the stockholders and Wall Street. This investment arm supplies the operating funds by those who seek a high return on their investment, with as much security as possible. These factors eventually force those willing to play the game of corporate survival to short-cut ethical responsibility thinking for the short-term result.

Over thirty-five percent of our nation's minority children are currently receiving an inadequate education or dropping out before graduating high school because of our misappropriated priorities. With our public education's financial funding dependent upon a healthy economy and tax base comes the question of who will be the future providers in this 21st Century? And who will be able to pay for the goods and services being produced, as our minorities will be in the majority in the next forty years?

With the future projected to decrease the need to utilize Americans in the world of physical labor little thought is produced on the screen or written page, the picture of what our future world will resemble other than being a world dealing with ill-educated people. Also ignored is the reality that the Earth's resources are finite, that even with all known reserves, the human population will eventually be out of potable water and oil. We are not adept in our recognition that there are growing separations and class divisions globally, divisions with the potential of causing a major threat to our way of life with the potential of producing more numerous 911's.

The interpretations of where we are and are going in this vista, range from an eventual Armageddon with increasing human despair and death through some cataclysmic event or catastrophic disease; to a futuristic world with planetary exploitation with all of us experiencing happy, quality lives, living lives of leisure motivated by human enterprise. Where we will be in this projection is dependent upon our overall health and how much money we have in the bank, laying the foundations of our current thinking and growing class divisions.

Our recent history shows that the foundations of accelerated greed and governing malfeasance occurred while we were young children. As we were riding our bikes and playing "cowboys and Indians", our government, coming out of the Second World War, infused borrowed money into the nations economy to jump-start our peacetime production. The purpose was to create domestic employment for the returning war veterans and generate livable incomes for America. While it was successful in this "jump-start" it also laid the groundwork of our current apathy, and the acceptance of a "progress at any cost" mentality.

Interstate highways constructed during the late 1950s through the 1960s induced new human cores of re-locations from city to country, giving birth to our suburbia and our growing dependence on the automobile. Military and government spending on manufacturing, education, and research created a strong, educated middle class building weapons of conflict. With this economic growth we were then distracted, then nurtured into a consumer mentality. Our income and spending habits grew into need for governing program intervention. We then accepted through this buyoff, governing inefficiencies and "pork-barrel" politicking creating the foundations of our current indebtedness.

Concurrent with the growth and the new cost of larger government spending came the business need of short-term profit taking. Corporate manipulations of political decision-making became the norm. The convenience store and shopping mall came into vogue, providing us with nearby receptacles for our cash, artificially affecting the short-term profit curve of the business world.

The banking and insurance industries driven by the need for quarterly profit introduced credit financing, because we did not have enough spending power to pay for all that was being produced. The credit card then combined the marketing and advertising expertise of Madison Avenue, utilizing a future promise to pay. The Exxon, McDonald's and Polaroid companies et al introduced new product and thinking into mainstream America, eventually permeating the entire globe. All companies, large and small, were then managed by the philosophy of John Keynes capitalism to profit in the short-term at the expense to our moral souls. In this, we were provided with the underlying belief that there was to be no end to the progress that could be undertaken by what we could consume.

We started to think that we were pretty smart and could buy ourselves out of any problem. We hit our country's apex with this explosive era, with our and the world's economy becoming dependent upon our consumptive habits and short attention span. It created the early conditioning of massive consumption, leading us into this modern day economy supported by our personal debt, monitored by our credit lines. While we were enjoying the bounty from this harvest, our nation's moral and financial underpinnings were being politically undermined.

Our government's originators provided a government that was supposedly for and by the people. This document initiated a three-tiered system, the executive, and the legislative and judicial branches with checks and balances to assure that no one entity would control the other. It did not anticipate nor plan for a fourth branch's impact on the process. Our special interests' and PAC groups now total over 4,000 in number and are paid to purchase the decisions of our leaders, not concerned with the overall needs of America.

One does not have to be a CPA or numbers expert to understand the tremendous financial pressures on the middle and lower economic classes of our country's population. Sixty-one percent of all our homes are supported by two incomes earning less percentage-wise than they earned in 1983. More than 70% of the country's population makes less than $45,000 a year.

Our headlines today are filled with the growing numbers of the new unemployed and their emotional reactions on a daily basis. There are human faces, hearts and minds represented behind each column of these numbers. Each figure multiplied by the family members being caught in the downsizing of Middle America.

Twenty-five years ago the typical family of four had a combined median income of $17,800. Today this couple's averages hover around $42,000 annually, if both parents are still employed. Suppose this family is smarter than the norm. One or both adults work an extra job if they can find the work they are educated to do, or are managing their own business. They watch their expenses and budget their income, limiting their purchases, building for their future. On the surface, everything should be fine in this equation. But, there are four economic realities the family unit has to face to survive living in this country. The cost of living the "American Dream" is now unaffordable to the middle-class family in America.

Today the average home costs over $137,000. With 20% down ($27,400) and closing costs of 1.5 points, the family is faced with monthly payments of $700 a month for thirty years with annual payments totaling (rentals in many communities are approximately the same) **$8,400.**

Our transportation and domestic car leasing associations report that it now costs 42 cents a mile to operate one medium-sized vehicle (fuel, monthly payment, maintenance, insurance, etc.) With an average distance traveled annually of 15,000 miles totals (just for one car) **$6,300.**

Food with lunches out, realistically $130.00 per week, totals **$6,760.**

Taxes — National, state and local for the year with Social Security, Medicaid, and Medicaid included. (27.3% + withholding) totals **$17,640.**

TOTAL **$39,100.**

This leaves this above average family with a small balance to pay for all other general expenses. Costs which include utilities and credit card debt, continued education, family health and insurance, a second car, clothing, saving and spending to propel the economy, while bailing out our nation's growing indebtedness. This same family can live in less expensive housing or apartments, drive an older car and live on simpler menu, reducing their overhead. They can start some type of home business in the service industry for a potential tax write-off and add to their personal education to try to stay ahead of the curve, but they won't find, in their near future, jobs that will pay a livable income based upon their current expertise.

Place your take-home pay on paper and multiply this number by the pay periods you will have over the next twelve months. Then list all your deductions and interest expenses, rent or mortgage, food and utilities and your car payments for the year. Then add to this the insurance for your home and car (include your gas costs) and your state and local taxes (include sales tax), Medicaid and Medicare and Social Security deductions. Then add your other expenses, like clothing, movies, children's school materials, lunches and TV cable and include your credit card debt. Then subtract this number from your total net income for the period and see how much you have left to invest for your retirement.

In the last two decades, a foreign employee who works more hours for much less has displaced the blue and white-collar middle-class wage earner. What that worker earns for the entire day presently equals one hour of wages of ours. And this same person is in the process of being replaced by technology and computers that are able to perform more accurately with less business expense.

The stress in one's eyes and the desperation of possibly being caught in a company downsizing, tells the story if one is sensitive to look. The world is awash in too many people desperate for jobs providing management with exploitable labor for additional business income. Sixty percent of the world's population, according to the United Nations, is vastly under-employed and also needs money to live.

The middle-class element of our recent past, which provided hope for the poor and a growing, strong profit base for business growth is now unraveling at the seams, creating an interesting scenario. Will our leadership provide the futuristic vision to address this transition with prudent common sense, keeping in mind our political divisions on how we do things? Will it also address what we personally expect because of government commitments, and at the same time accommodate our corporate world's mentality for the need to profit short-term?

With our changing expectations it is difficult, if not impossible, to support a monthly mortgage payment or rent and rising family costs when the growing job base is paying less than $40,000 per year. As America's middle-class is becoming no longer cost-effective by the business community, do we eventually drop our standard of living to the rest of the world? Or, harder yet, with all the problems we are faced with — do we develop long-term corporate and governing compassion in bringing theirs collectively up to ours?

We are experiencing increasing numbers of terrorist attacks, worldwide bankruptcies, family breakdowns, with one out of five of our children living in poverty and hunger, with a teenager becoming the typical parent, or committing suicide. And a newly forming corporate America not perceiving that, with diminishing income of the buying public, who will be able to afford what they are producing? These human and economic realities are placing us in a future major bind and are adding to our current stress levels.

According to our numerous psychiatric studies compiled by our mental health experts, roughly 10% of our nation's population, or 28 million people living next to us, are suffering some form of mental or emotional disease. These are individuals who are hurting and disillusioned with an absence of hope and self-worth. It does not take much to push one over the edge as evidenced by the bombings in Oklahoma and New York City, mass public shootings, a mother drowning her children, or some disgruntled lunatic mailing anthrax-laced letters to some unsuspecting addressee.

We hear about or experience the results of once productive persons becoming so frustrated, so filled with hatred, that they are able to walk into the office place or neighborhood store and kill a number of people. We spend more than $28,000 a year placing and keeping a person in jail, with little or no personal rehabilitation, while as a nation we invest or waste (depending upon one's point of view) less than six thousand dollars per year in educating each of our school children.

Over 80% of our prison population has been abused as children and never finished high school, with the cycle definitely escalating. 60% of this same number short cut the learning process for the quick reality escapes of dealing drugs to make an income. We now find ourselves in the mode of over-reacting to the symptoms by building more prisons with more bureaucracy and its additional overhead costs.

One can empathize when he or she is involved personally, or has a friend, or family member, on a fixed income faced with new taxes or huge medical invoices, or loses a child too early in life. For others there is nothing more dangerous than a person unemployed with little opportunity to feed oneself. Desperation leads into disastrous decisions, with those persons easily influenced by religious leanings and the basic needs of human survival. This projected picture shows a reduced income for Middle America with the poor getting poorer and rich becoming more affluent, with the future becoming more life threatening.

It is a growing process of human separation that is presenting us with some very difficult challenges with few compassionate governing options. If we are unable to re-establish the middle class firmly with political urgency we will all experience the negatives together. Looking at the near future, without the existence of a strong, global, middle class buffer, it looks as if the rich will eventually receive the bill. With the coming of the "New World Order" the walls will never be high enough to ever be personally secure, as we learned on the morning of September 11, 2001.

****

The psychological world defines reality as what we perceive it to be at a specific moment in time. Our minds take in all of our surroundings, digesting what our body senses and translates this into what we believe is the truth. When a dentist comes at us with a drill we either develop a fear of potential pain, creating pain, or we can place ourselves into another point of reference, eliminating any discomfort through another illusion. Our prisoners of war during the Viet Nam era, when asked how they stayed sane after years of being enclosed in bamboo cages and tortured beyond what we can imagine, all responded that they put their minds in another place in time, often in prayer, creating a different reality.

There are those who believe that our current lives are this type of an illusion. That when we perceive that a pain or discomfort is going to happen, we defensively create an escape mechanism, ignoring the base cause of our true realities.

Since we have been conditioned all of our lives to perceive that what we have been doing is in the natural order of things, it is difficult to conceive that what we have been doing as a society is wrong. It is for this reason that the next few chapters will be a condensed version of some major events that have led into what we believe to be our current illusions and our basic truths.

If you are turned off by history text and basic fact I ask that you not bog yourself down with the words being used, but skip to Chapter XVIII for your edification. It is more upbeat, describing a plausible light at the end of the tunnel, with a few suggestions for what we can do with the rest of our lives, if and when, freely elected.

When our country was rediscovered in the late 1400s, man's development was governed by what he could see, sense and feel and intuitively imagine. (I use the word rediscovered because some of our historians now believe that if the Vikings weren't here approximately 450 years earlier that the Chinese definitely were, but that is another subject for another day.) Money and power were controlled by a king on another shore, bestowed to those he decided to reward through partisan relationships and the spoils of war.

The peasantry, who were kept poor, uneducated and scattered, provided the pleasures and conveniences in life for the upper class. Their existence was governed by the shortsighted agendas of those with wealth, power and control. Human nature being what it is, life for those without was short and hazardous.

These two class divisions led into human despair with revolt increasing the need of additional expenditures for weapons and armies of warfare. With the widening differences of living standards of these human conditions and the financial drain of the military came the constants of rebellion and terrorism, creating the need to survive at any sacrificial cost. If we are inclined to think about the world's conditions today, this same scenario is being duplicated but on a larger, more intense and escalating global scale of economic divisions.

We question why we are called the "Ugly American," so disliked and oftentimes hated by others we have helped in the past. We do not comprehend the use of the word "arrogant" or realize the destruction we cause under the guise of trying to assist others in need. Our perceived benevolence in addressing the evils and need in this world through our largeness and good will are more than offset by our nation's global agendas of corporate greed and contrivances for wealth and market control.

While we support over 25% of the world's benevolence through U.N. services with less than six percent of the Earth's population, we in this country consume more than a third of all of the world's industrial output annually. Our lifestyles create a resentment of the Second and Third Worlds who envy our wealth and standards of living, but brand us for believing in our self-entitlements at their personal expense.

We are not taught to understand the hardships of those around this globe, others who are easily manipulated through their emotional perceptions conditioned by what they are told. Nor are we aware of foreign leadership who personally resent our being on the "top of the hill," suspicious of our nation's global agendas. The human tendency is to rebel against being manipulated and controlled by an outsider, or resist change through force, eventually despising the intruder.

G500 corporate institutions today manage more than half of all the financial wealth generated by the world's business communities globally, according to financial statistics and tracked through the Internet. American banks, insurance, oil and food companies dominate Second and Third World politics managed by executives who are not able to relate to the needs of the average world citizen. More than 60% of the world's population is un-, or under-employed, living annually on less income than the average American earns in a week. Idle time, poverty and human ignorance allow an easy manipulation of the masses by but a handful of persons taking advantage of their hunger and need for immediate survival.

The colonization of the world by the world powers of England, Spain, Portugal and France left historical levels of human devastation and resentment for wealth and control. These same factors are not only being duplicated today under the guise of addressing the world's many ills, but accelerated because of our speeding age of technology on a global scale.

Whoever supplies one in need with the promise of salvation, or a meal to stave off starvation, or a gun to take from another, will derive a form of human loyalty similar to a household's pet, conditioned to respond to the one who feeds, nurtures and protects them. There are growing numbers of conditioned zealots who use this method, controlling the masses to riot, revolt and war. All use hunger, poverty and ignorance as their controlling and motivating forces.

We would react the same as any individual around the world if we were in their position with foreigners invading our native shores, to the point where we would do almost anything at the first chance for defense or revenge. When combining human desperation with the manipulations of religion, a possible spiritual atonement is then added into this equation.

Through this comes a molding acceptance of leaving a harsh life with no hope, to the perception of receiving a heavenly reward. These persons are then brainwashed and conditioned into developing a "kamikaze mentality", creating a domestic genocide of Jonestown, the terrorist bombings in Jerusalem, or the Middle Eastern pilots committing suicide, crashing into buildings, sacrificing their lives, in the name of God.

Today our evolution is in a historic, explosive duplication of Columbus' time, with declining opportunities for America's middle class and the dangers of this world's increasing populations. Our current reality is that our life-systems are delicately balanced through laser beams, mirrors, smoke, and our public perceptions that somehow we will escape this truth. Out of this it is important to realize that if one has a productive job in a safe neighborhood providing for his or her family, that person would be less likely to sacrifice his or her possessions and secular lives to prematurely enter Heaven. Likewise, if each of us were cognizant of one God who is loving and concerned about all of His children equally, we would be coexisting in a less dangerous, emotionally driven and splintered world.

This century is also like no other, because we have the opportunity to learn from our past utilizing the speed of technology to revise this path we are traveling. With this instrument we can massively retool who and what we want to be, and through this evolution create a new way of thinking and God willing, a better world. We can go to the origins of our many problems, understanding the many issues as part of the whole. Then from this, create a plan of action that will absorb our variables of human nature anticipating our emotional outbursts. And to realize that, no matter how well one plans, that some unseen event will rear its ugly head throwing out the best of one's intentions.

CHAPTER VII
HISTORICAL REPETITIONS

Thirty years ago, I was involved in managing a small division of a large manufacturing company in the health and beauty aid field. I was good at what I did and moved up the management food chain quickly, feeding my male ego and pride. In my mid-twenties, I had the responsibility for a thirty-one state area and traveled extensively, experiencing the beauty and business challenges of this nation of ours. Deep down I think that I truly enjoyed the hunt, the chase and conquest of the deal. It was, in this reflection, similar to our ancestral predecessors chasing down the wooly mammoths to fill the belly, generating immediate reward no matter the personal cost.

My thinking then was centered on the maneuverings that I would use to consummate my next business transaction, instead of noticing the growing social problems of the times. That was our conditioning then, to work and play hard focusing on one's needs, to cut corners, to be smarter than our competition while building for our personal futures. In this we were gradually assimilated by this battle into our acquired materialism, and an assumption that others would eventually create a better world for us and in turn for our offspring. In this transition, we became sheep in a flock following something so empty and shallow, now evolved into what we are thinking today.

I remember my childhood as a time when life for many in the middle class was flowing smoothly, with most persons treated with dignity and respect. It was a time of innocence when families, businesses, government services, social organizations and churches had definite roles in developing our human behavior.

Each sector had its shared ethical responsibilities with political and business decisions, to a large degree, made to benefit the entire nation and our locales collectively. Company employees had loyalty to management and management to their employees. There was greed and corruption in business and government then as now, but living today has accelerated the outfalls with greased palms and our distorted personal expectations of seeking financial security through any means.

Many of our generation were fortunate to have been raised in family surroundings that provided the sound foundations of childhood. We had the early luxury of a two-parent, two-gender introduction, hopefully preparing us for the normal challenges of living life. We managed to overcome most obstacles, the normal ups and downs that most of us shared while we are growing up. We learned how to eat solid food, tie our own shoes and even developed a work ethic while thinking for ourselves. In this we learned that the value of things that we labored for, were far more important to us than something received with little or no effort.

What we purchased from this sweat equity we took care of religiously, which is not part of our overall current domestic conditioning. As we acquired our perceived necessities over our years, we were conditioned to want more, more money and other things from our government services. In this we lost the larger purpose of self-reliance, not appreciating the values and hard work it takes to support a functioning democracy.

Today there is no accountability of leadership to address things with common cause. Our government's bureaucracy and our politicians have been conditioned into a posturing mode of partisan conflict, not able to embrace the much larger responsibilities we have as humankind to our Creator.

Our democratic methods of placing leadership in positions of power are similar to using different playbooks and coaches in each quarter of a football game and constantly changing the rules as the game is being played. With different operating guidelines changing with whomever is in power, comes tremendous waste of talent, energies and finances. The special interests' attempt to sway decisions and priorities by changing their methods each election period, but stay focused on their overall objectives. This places those we elect to lead us at a dismal disadvantage. The world we have today is filled with too many broken programs and the inefficiencies of our government leaders, their existence dependent upon our short memory spans.

Our election process, by its nature, forces eventual social and moral costs with the breakdown in continuity. In this we are not prepared for the changing dynamics of our times or the overall expense of our county's misdirection.

We do not want to comprehend the magnitude of the damage we have accomplished in such a short time, or the future expense of our nation's many serious problems. Our life chain and perceptions of current events today is the driven by-product of synthesized politics and corporate manipulation for dollar volume development and political control. We are in the awakening stages of realizing that our fragile resources of democratic governing are structured for building individual power and turf protection; the needs of the Earth and us becoming damned by this process we call governing ourselves.

Recorded history has shown that people have an inherent instinct to survive through their ingenuity, to move onto something new gaining from the experience when something is failing. In this, our nation's predecessors developed the ability to overcome their personal fears and the hidden agendas of others to provide for the bigger needs of what would become our Nation at large.

Five hundred years ago, Europe was coming off the throes of war, experiencing a major recession, similar to our times today. The different crowns, both victors and losers, were looking for ways to replenish their personal wealth and respond to the growing domestic need of their populations. In one of these countries an Italian sailor, an excellent salesman, was able to entice Spain's queen to part with some start-up capital investment to finance a new venture. Although he and she didn't know exactly where he was going or how much it would cost, the Spanish crown supplied the ships and personnel with the understanding that the plunder would benefit the crown and eventually this Italian.

When the colonists later migrated into this newly discovered land (the result of this business enterprise), they were escaping political and religious persecution from their homelands. They were able to survive through their ingenuity and to the trusting graciousness of the American native and our Father, using their intuitive native skills and a much smaller form of local government.

Over the years, America's populations grew, spreading south and west, requiring the need for legal conformity to bridge the many conflicting interpretations of governing law. With this growth came the desire for a formal political system to keep us from damaging each other, man being who he is.

With heavy debate our country's founders were able to initiate a complex yet simple governing philosophy known as our current Constitution and Bill of Rights. In this they wanted to avoid the hierarchy and corruptions of their past, fearful of a governmental largeness growing out of the control of the common people. In transitioning a concept into reality they trusted within themselves, relying on the power of God for a moral guidance combined with a continuous flow of wisdom and human compassion. But with man's historic inability to take what was a positive progress for humankind, we, over the past 50 years, have inadvertently allowed a transformation into what our founders initially feared. Today is replicating a fiefdom mentality, which we perceive as a functioning Democracy.

We are finally becoming aware of this situation and our larger truths generated not only by our past history, but also from our complex domestic and global difficulties via the Internet and cable news. Through this immediate information highway, we are now absorbing the outfall of what we have created causing much of our personal frustration. The upside is that we are finally learning that we have a history of ignoring the root causes of our problems, consistently treating the symptoms, not the original cause.

When you see a person in the grocery store using a credit card to acquire food you realize that America has serious problems. Today the average family needs a piece of plastic and line of credit to place nourishment on the table and support the roof over their heads. The result of this distraction is that if a person can't afford a pair of pants, it is difficult to think about the price of a pair of shoes; or for the average citizen dealing with the growing financial stress of each day to think out the issues of governing reform or addressing the increasing problems of this Earth.

Historically, we repeat the constants of overcoming bondage with the courage to change then allow the evolution of events to lead into freedom and abundance. But we also make the constant error of allowing this abundance to develop into apathy and waste, a process, which again leads into bondage with constant human setbacks causing this historical recycling of events. Each generation, as does ours, has had its opportunities to break this cycle. Most if not all to this time have failed miserably, which is our current challenge to alter.

What we do from this time forward will determine our children's future destiny and the Earth's overall health for all time. We can either keep on doing what we are doing, accelerating our many current mistakes and problems or address what we have with some faith and common sense, financial practicality. According to the experts who do our nation's planning, the future projects that a large number of us in this country won't be needed for domestic production. Even with our political tampering with the global economy via NAFTA and AFTA and the Euro currencies there will be no short-term benefits for the average American.

As evidenced by each day's news, negative events are accelerating in an upward spiral with time becoming blurred in its evolution and human toll. We are finding that in this process we no longer have a common enemy, other than ourselves not being able to focus on the larger purpose of human life. It seems that we are now part of a Hemlock Society in the heated process of silently putting our support systems to death, with few concerned with the eventual outcome.

Each of us now is being challenged to think things through and break this historical repetition of our self-flagellations. The impact of what we will be transferring to our children, instead of bringing this world into harmony, is the complexity that is currently tearing us apart. There are now one hundred and ninety nations in their own form of human evolution, adding to our many human divisions, oftentimes building into turf and regional wars, terrorism and genocide.

Over the past 50 years of our lives our government, the United Nations, private insurance underwriters, our non profit foundations and the business community have financed tens of thousands of studies to get a "supposed" handle on our and the world's many problems. The thoughts for, or the implementations of, a peaceful change are hampered by the lack of future focus on where we are going and what we eventually want to become. The current assimilation of using these findings is ineffective because political realities do not incorporate the human spirit factor of addressing adversity with a sensitive compassionate overview. Not one anticipates the natural fact that people are afraid of the intervention of outsiders and the unknown.

As most governments, including ours, are thoughtfully structured so no one is held personally responsible, the political process becomes mired in inefficiency, far removed from utilizing common sense. Because of this, senior political policy makers rely on the safety of numbers rather than risk revolutionary individual thought, ignoring the full responsibilities of leadership. As a result, we have the history of accepting this process of blindly following our elected generals often without delving into their personal agendas.

We are now beginning to realize that we have been traveling on a ship without a rudder, no game plan, and no shared vision to let us know how to fix things together. With the exception of God's Ten Commandments, our Constitution and Bill of Rights, we have never had an explained moral road map to collectively follow, understanding the rules of the game, the experience we call human life.

In the grander scheme, of all living things, we are the new kids on the block. We are in an immediate need of having our diaper changed. What we have is soiled and messy and drooping around our knees. We are, at times, adults on the surface behaving as a child in an irrational manner, taking our psychological stresses out on each other against our parent's wishes. Not too long ago our political leadership did not address or anticipate the small problems we had with checks and balances, and long-term thinking. Those small global and human problems then, because of the absence of anticipatory planning, are our major problems today.

We are in need of contemplating a re-engineering and structure that will let us know simply where we are going, what the rules will be, and how we would mutually benefit from our involvement, creating positive global results and a kinder and gentler world for our children. We should also be appreciative that we are not alone in this walk of confrontation and reinventing ourselves, as each generation has its challenges and becomes stronger from each period's demands and dilemmas. All countries worldwide are in the same format of initially understanding the magnitude of Earth's many problems and dealing involuntarily with chaotic change.

As this is being written, the once Soviet Union and the Communist-bloc countries are now massively reorganizing the failures of past governing mismanagement with few financial resources. Africa, the Middle East and India are facing the difficulties of addressing human rights, ignorance, the shortage of jobs, food and drinkable water and the increase of incurable disease. Our Southern neighbors in Central and South America are in the upheaval of reformulating their corruptive dictatorial challenges, drug production and regional warfare. Japan is confronted with economic and political upheaval, nearing bankruptcy, in attempting to deal with the politics and pressures of the rest of the world as an island country. China is confronted with blending the forces of capitalism and Communism in an overpopulated and ecologically stressed country. Our European counterparts are attempting to establish a unified process of governing trade and politics with Germany absorbing the problems of unification and moral corruption. All of us worldwide are in the same boat of trying to make sense out of our common disorders with the decline of the global ecology, as our one secular commonality.

We, together, can address our many challenges with intelligent, thoughtful programming inducing simplified change, or allow a major catastrophe to happen. The difficulty is that these catastrophes and challenges have and will continually happen. All the environmental, financial, social, spiritual and political disasters we have today are accelerating in intensity and number.

The following words and concept are structured to have us think out future change and eventually commit to listen to our inner voice of reasoning. To take the time to reach inside each one of us to determine the future of our nation and eventually this planet, Earth. For where we are today is far removed from what our parents or ourselves envisioned when we entered this world not too long ago. The major advantage we have over our ancestors' time is that we can share, then blend, our knowledge and concerns globally. To form a larger public awareness through the printed word then digest what we sense through our hearts, our minds, and our intuitive souls.

When we take the time to think about things getting better we oftentimes think about and pray for God's intervention. We also, at times, will question what spiritually motivates us to do what we do. Each of us would like to find an inner serenity and purpose for our lives, filled with peace and prosperity. We would like to believe that all that we do today will eventually result in security for our individual families. Through this, we hope that the future will provide for a better existence for each of our children. This hope will be the common-thread in what you are about to read.

CHAPTER VIII
DECELERATION

Numerous articles written over the years have reported that we are the most litigious nation on this Earth. The United States now possesses over 90% of all practicing attorneys worldwide, according to our U.S. census and U.N. tracking. Our universities and law schools will graduate, in the next ten years, twice the number currently practicing law, analyzing our current enrollment. Presently there is one attorney for each 326 adult citizens residing in our country.

There are now over 5,000 bills waiting to be placed on the floors of Congress for arbitration and debate that may become new demands to be enforced. There are over 850,000 encyclopedia sized books of rules in existence that govern what we do, how we act and are punished, trying to govern our human responses. Not one adequately addresses this effect on our human emotions.

Our technological advances, created over the last ten years, are able to replicate the information structure of the past 200 years in less than two minutes of visual stimulation and "sound bites." Mankind's industrial advancement of the last 2000 years has been duplicated in the last two years since its introduction. What used to take several days and weeks to learn is now measured in teraflops, or trillionths of seconds of lapsed time today.

Through this we are able to compute the vast majority of world events at a speed accelerated beyond the average human's capacity to emotionally and mentally digest. In mind numbing and speeding quantities, wars that used to take years to resolve now are completed in less than 100 days while we sit transfixed to the activity through the television screens in our homes. Simultaneously, as these "hundred-day wars" are taking place, thousands of billions of dollars are invested on Wall Street, for profit or loss, in less time than it takes to blink one's eye. We are becoming blurred in our understanding of each event's effect on our perceptions and psyches. Today, because of our electronic infrastructure, our situation has evolved into our expectations of receiving immediate answers.

We have not had the time to cope rationally to this dramatic effect, or to think things through before we do them anyway. Information is now available in huge gigabytes of memory and teraflops of speed overwhelming the human senses in coping with this acceleration, producing our current terminology of "road rage" and our acceptance of global carnage. The subconscious fallout; we are becoming insensitive to human values and quality of life, losing our focus as human beings.

Barings P.L.C., WorldCom, Texaco and Enron failed because of greed and insider manipulation of financial numbers and derivatives being dealt in a "junk-bond" format. Tens of thousands of investors lost hundreds of billions of dollars in an eye-blink of time, destroying many lifetimes of saving. Decisions are now so evolved that the futures of entire countries are being jeopardized and composed in brief seconds, by insiders not appreciating the human side and the destructive nature of greed. The world's entire financial health is nearing collapse, being dealt away by human faces that are disappearing by the push of a button.

Vast numbers of professionals and business owners are working 65-70 hours a week with more intensity and harder than ever before, with increasing stress in their eyes with heart attacks increasing in their numbers. Children, through the use of electronic games, are learning how to kill in a horrendous manner and are exposed to pornography and the illicit sex of pedophiles. Companies driven by quarterly returns are now justified in using these tools to constantly adjust and downsize people's lives, with four persons now replacing a work force of 400 five years ago.

Never in recorded time has man evolved a technology so widely used in a world experiencing the throes of self-destruction. We are living in an acceleration of time becoming blind-sighted by our emotional reactions to a lot of trivia and false truths. We have become addicted into an immediate gratification mode, with our anxieties growing, our decisions driven emotionally.

The result of this is that we have lost the ability to think things through, not taking time to understand a problem's originating history, or its cause and effect. We are now becoming blinded into accepting things as they are, following non-visionary leaders with our larger purpose as humankind becoming lost somewhere in cyberspace. In this we (consciously and subconsciously) are experiencing the middle steps of a corporate meltdown of human life and in turn, our comfort zones in accommodating this alteration.

Today, our shrinking world is in an angry human confrontation with many people fighting for their personal existence to have their anxieties heard. All one has to do to experience this transference is to watch the human interaction in a traffic jam or office place; the human mass entering or exiting as if they were traveling the path of ants in an anthill, snapping at each other's face. Our 21st century is creating the need for new thought and expressive new thinking to absorb this transition. It could trigger our main downfall or if used as a tool for a self-healing, create a rebirth of our nation. This could provide the initial staging area for our future survival, combining God's presence with this explosive era of technology.

Over the past four decades while we, as a society, sought to embrace this world of technological advancement, we have minimized the importance of God and His unconditional love. In the past, human survival was more dependent upon God working through man, rather than man working on God. In this tradeoff, we entered into a mental zone of mass confusion about our individual roles and the responsibilities we have while living on the Earth.

We are duplicating a history of sometimes moving forward, doing things a little bit smarter, thinking that we are making our lives better, but more often, when we step back from the fray, we find that we are pacing ourselves backwards, losing more of the intuitive purposes of our lives. Out of this it seems that we have missed an exit sign somewhere not too long ago.

Because of the combinations of these two worlds, Gods message-making and our information highway, we are just beginning to understand the separate life stages that each of us are traveling together. We are now living a time that is creating the foundations of identifying who we really are and where we are going, while identifying our many options as a global society.

We have a history of sometimes slowing down through prayer and meditation, placing our needs into our Father's time frame and hearing what is being said. In this journey, we blend in what we intuitively know with our mutual concerns listening to God for direction. This, in turn, allows our individual belief systems to grow with wisdom and knowledge, which broadens the depth of our understanding. Through prayer and silently listening, all of us have the ability to receive direction in everything we do, if we are willing to silently hear what is being said.

When I was in my late teens and early 20s, time was digestible in movement with us more in harmony with the energies of this Earth. Many of the problems of the world held little weight in one's thinking compared to having food on the table or a roof over one's head, or living peaceably with one's neighbor. A person could live their entire lives in this country never knowing the plight of the ecology or the poverty of the Third World. We were able to understand our local and national events in a more digestible humane format.

We subscribed to daily, weekly and monthly publications to keep abreast of what was going on in our hometowns, nationally and around the globe. With this information we were able to formulate our own ideas, developing our own conclusions and our own inner truths. We realized that each article was written with an agenda, but were able to balance this by examining each issue through the varying eyes of each writer.

The pros and cons of each situation were presented, allowing the reader the time to understand each issues' "cause and effect", looking at the many sides of each subject in an more objective manner. In this, we were able to develop our own perceptions of each situation, separating fact from fiction, good information from the bad. Today, we are bombarded with massive amounts of trivia and intended misinformation, clouding the actual picture of what is being developed.

Because of this, we are being forced to deal with a new untested chapter of mankind's evolution, digesting this world around us misconstrued with partial truths and hidden agendas. It is a test in dealing with a global economy enriching but a handful of persons, the forerunner of a new world government motivated by greed and massive human control. This is a foreign thought for many of us, as we are not formally trained to understand the larger dynamics of this type of world, anticipating the future fallout and human cost of what is transpiring.

We live in a democracy that has been remolded in recent times, by a larger political agenda structured to convince us that almost everything is politically and secularly fixable. In this we relinquished the larger responsibilities of self-reliance.

Out of this we have the evolved perception that most, if not all, of our personal problems and mistake making can be repaired through the passages of Congressional bills and massive money spending in four-year presidential cycles. We then go through the motions of a democratic voting procedure hoping little damage will be done and then complain a lot when we learn the convoluted truth or are negatively affected.

The strength of our founder's original concept of a pure democracy incorporated the avenues of human co-operation and if not satisfied with the performance of our leadership and local representatives, having the option of electing someone else. The weakness is that they never envisioned the political inroads and control that would be exploited by corporate America. Today we are being led by a handful of legal minds conditioned for conflict resolution, not peaceful arbitration in dealing with our internal social problems. The outcome is political specimens supported by lobbyists who spend hundreds of millions of dollars purchasing our political decisions.

While it can be argued that the past 50 years created a well paid, middle-class society and equality has made its inroads; the downside is that Washington's inner workings, and we, have become accustomed to wasting trillions of dollars supporting our entitlements and the numerous hidden agendas of "pork-barrel" legislation. Over the same years, our society, including our religious bodies, never did adjust to the start of this negative transition or the human cost of their financial add-ons.

With the "Guns and Butter" diplomacy of the mid 1960s, we did not comprehend the loss of our national and family values while we were making a living. In this short period, as we were handling our day-to-day responsibilities, our government slowly mandated God and common sense to be taken out of our governing infrastructure and soon after, our public schools. In this we cost our following generations their moral grounding and the larger use of our working minds. Nor did we notice during this same time, that our democratic procedures were being taken over by special interests representing the needs of their corporate clients. Combined this transference of control nurtured our current government into becoming our abusive, surrogate parent.

Our financial and human wastes today are mind-boggling and tragic. Military bases and government buildings built over the past 50 years are being destroyed because they are deemed antiquated and not cost effective. There is little thinking that if rehabilitated these structures would have the strong potential in providing each locale with affordable retrofitted housing units, schools and office buildings. Instead they are politically dismissed and transformed by wrecking crew into a pile of buried trash, reflective of our consumptive habits of use, abuse and discard.

City and county governments and land developers use tax supported bond monies to construct sports and shopping centers to benefit private enterprise. Unneeded roads leading to nowhere and expensive government complexes built with cost over-runs are not regulated or the offenders penalized. Medical costs are skyrocketing and are unaffordable to the average citizen, and the list goes on; with several thousand ecological disasters crying out for attention while our society creates more new billionaires taking from what our system offers. The private sector profited handsomely from the 1960s through our current times, but we lost our nation's moral and ethical grounding while we were distracted in our chase for the "All American Dream".

Our children's generation is now faced with paying the future escalating costs of what we, their parents, have allowed to be created. Many understand the overall situation, as they don't see a positive outcome. They are disillusioned, frustrated and angry, a growing number losing respect for us, the adults in their world. Dropouts, teenage suicide and drug sales are rampant. Our streets are imploding with anarchy and gangs with children killing each other. This generation is crying out for parenting skills that few adults are in position to supply. Our country is overpopulated with too many people not having the ability to be liable.

We are now on a treadmill leading into an abyss, surrounded by a growing insanity that is going faster and faster beyond human comprehension. We, together, are permitting long-term carnage for immediate gain at an accelerated rate of exchange. We have become a one-hour Christian nation seeking the comfort of a drive through religious service far removed from grasping the larger responsibilities of maintaining a working democracy.

Because of our secular diversions and political decisions spread over our years, we have created our now fragile existence, never quite functioning on all eight cylinders of our society's main engine. For all of the above reasons, and our current and past history, the balance of what you will read are but a few suggestions for your personal thought for responsible change.

There are not too many of us who would be inclined to read a 3000 page dissertation filled with facts and numbers with few, if any, pictures to prove a point. For that reason this book is short and generalized in its descriptions of our many problem's complex origins. For any single person to think that they may have the answers to our many difficulties would be considered arrogant and irresponsible. But collectively we have the answers to all that surrounds us within reach of our fingertips.

CHAPTER IX
AWAKENINGS

While we, of our generation, were dealing with the pressures of growing up, the rest of the world was in its own overt form of chaos and disorder. With President Kennedy's assassination came a major loss of our childlike innocence, thrown into a world of adult insanities. Many of us believed that Camelot went down the drain with his departure. We were then overtly emptied of our hopes and dreams, losing sight of our idealistic direction. In this, one of the few opportunities that history provides in having a visionary leader was lost to an unproven conspiracy, leading into our current world of lost energies and massive corporate greed. During the 1960s, while we were experiencing the politically manipulated conflicts of Viet Nam, the needs of our country's poor and uneducated population were massive and divisive.

At the time the Johnson Administration was in the process of politically mandating undeclared wars on all fronts — poverty, segregation and the Vietnamese — the Supreme Court decided that a child could be bussed across entire counties to balance our ethnic mix, and self-prescribed racial divisions. This mandate to integrate our public schools and therefore each community, though for humane reasons, ignored the fact that several thousands of years of human conditioning were being legally altered overnight.

It did not absorb the reality that the average U.S. citizen was not formally educated to comprehend the past history of racial inequality, or develop solutions to overcome our socioeconomic separateness with compassionate civility. Instead of accommodating, then implementing a peaceful transition based on educating the public of the cause and effect, the human will to rebel out of ignorance surfaced.

Our news reports were filled with the pent up hatreds of race divisions with governors carrying baseball bats, the peace marches in Alabama and Mississippi with K.K.K. induced lynching and human genocide; a response of a small but vocal vehement minority. To compound this tragedy, these same judiciaries took prayer out of our public lives in the mid-1960s, leading us into our loss of our nation's moral direction leading into our current conflicts of religious interpretation in our schools.

Concurrently, illegal drugs made their inroads producing "the biggest bang for the buck", introducing their escapes and artificially induced profit and death on the streets. Combined, a downward human spiral was constructed.

In this we lost our overall focus and moral direction as a caring self-responsible society, as with these diversions the private corporate business sector began to manipulate political decisions to profit its bottom line handsomely. Our perception of a working democracy was then breeched by President Nixon and the commission of Watergate.

This compounded our loss of innocence and faith in government action, mortally wounding our trust in our governing leadership. The foundations of today's financial beast and governing malfeasance were compounded during his tenure. Nixon took our nation's currency off of the gold standard, creating a fiat system. This birthed a valueless currency backed by future promises of worth with our government printing money with little value, other than the perceptions of big money investors and us, the country's citizens.

Following World War II, with the accelerations of government subsidized programs, more people were becoming conditioned to earn and want more during the 1960s. Because of this, with business profit as the prime motivator, we were then incorporated into the human mentality of never being satisfied. This initiated the driving forces of the convenience store being located in our backyard; television-sets becoming the prime marketing force, and the shopping mall having everything under one roof. This transition spread the urban population base into a massive suburb relocation program, displacing the tax base of our inner cities. This, in turn, created our dependence on the automobile and our increasing thirst for oil. All underwritten by deficit spending backed by a valueless currency.

Government spending on manufacturing, education and research then created a strong middle class dependent upon building weapons of conflict, creating the military-industrial complex. Our inner cities, and later suburban America absorbed the human transfer cost, leading into the realm of political maneuvering and a shallowness of neighborhood values generating the apathy that we have with our political world today.

From that point on, we were financially and then emotionally following non-visionary leadership, unable to anticipate the ramifications of what we were creating, a government and nation now running blatantly out of any moral control. Political decisions then became motivated with short-term campaign promises, dedicated to creating the illusion of a "feel good mentality", underwritten with deficit financing.

While we were experiencing our domestic problems of the volatile 1960s, the rest of the nations of the Earth were experiencing their own self-induced dysfunctions. On the opposite side of the world, China was hostile to outside interlopers with Mao willing to war to protect its borders from suspected U.S. intrusions while quelling an internal rebellion. The Soviet Empire concurrently had designs on controlling all of the assets and governments through Cold War confrontations with the Free World.

Western Europe was racked with political scandals and corruption rocking its regimes during a period of prosperity after recovering from the ravages of World War II. Latin America, Eastern Europe, African and Asian dictatorships were manipulated by the KGB & our CIA through bribery, military takeovers, political corruption and assassination of those in opposition.

Israel was involved in the Yom Kipper War with Lebanon, and the P.L.O. attempted to settle land, water and religious disputes through regional warfare. OPEC was created to retaliate against Israel and the "Seven Sisters" dictating monopoly for profit and product control. America's corporations were developing relationships with national heads of countries whose customs and populations they little understood for global distribution and financial control.

Iran was involved in a civil uprising with the Shah being displaced by Khomeini during the Carter years. The U.S. then backed Iraq and Saddam Hussein in a war against Iran, not understanding the distrust we would generate by negating our previously brokered financial and social commitments to the Iranian leader. Six thousand years of Middle Eastern history and our past political commitments were then ignored in our switching sides. This evolved in the following years into a suspicion of the true agendas and alliances of the United States.

In this short period political maneuverings and our foreign policy generated socioeconomic and cultural divisions. This in turn became manipulated by religious ideologies and despotic regimes, financially underwritten by our corporate need of oil.

Today each election period generates several billions of dollars of corporate donations to control future political posturing. The need for campaign financing corrupts the morals and larger purpose of the office holders and candidates in serving the actual needs of the general public and this nation of ours. These donations, under the guise of "hard and soft" political financial contributions, control political agendas eventually enhancing their private coffers and market control.

The presidential race of 2000 exceeded 600 million dollars in expenditures for a job that pays $400,000 a year. Expenditures for all political races exceeded 3.2 billion dollars this same election period. In New York, the mayoral race exceeded 83 million dollars with the House and Senate contests matching this excess. Millions invested for a position of authority and law making for a Congressman's salary of $150,000 per year. When a good-old-boy network can deliver a government program into the hands of a friend and business associate, the group mutually prospers at the expense of the larger population. The Iran and Watergate investigations conducted just a short time ago milked a 6-year period, with each generating over 33 million dollars in legal billings for the prosecution.

It is amazing how easily these numbers are recorded with but barely a whimper. When we were younger, a million, then a billion was an unheard of figure, mind numbing in their largeness. Now we have the word trillion becoming commonplace in our everyday language. That is a number with twelve zeros behind the starting number. With our "feel good at any cost" mentality we now have created a national indebtedness of 6.5 trillion dollars, or more than $24,000 for each one of us living in this country.

During this same period, Medicare, Medicaid, food stamps and housing programs were initiated, leaving a growing population dependent upon the taxpayer's goodwill and charity with few sweat-equity requirements. As it is human nature to take as much as one can with little or any effort, we are now in the process of trying to break this dependence after experiencing three generations dependant on the welfare of the taxpayers. As a result, we allowed our government and our court system to shatter the integrity and moral foundation of the United States. We also simultaneously experienced the largest corporate financial "sting" in all of recorded business history.

The average married couple in the early 1960s could buy a $12,000 home, a new $2,000 car and become a productive element in the workplace based upon sweat equity and intelligence. There was a parent at home, with few exceptions, to take care of the children at the end of the school day. Many may remember we were going to conquer the world of Communism (we did), solve the pressing issues of homelessness, illiteracy and racial prejudice (we didn't). We were also going to overcome sexual bias, hunger and discrimination via "The Great Society," through government programming — and the majority of us bought into it.

We, of our generation, believed or were led to perceive that all persons were to become healthy, environmentally conscious, successful in the world of business, get married and raise the all-American family, creating a better world for the majority. A person then had the opportunity to gain a quality education from a majority of teachers who, on the whole, loved their profession and taught children to think. We could also enjoy the great outdoors without being poisoned, and we could leave our house doors unlocked, able to trust those around us to leave things alone. While we were experiencing all of this, we lost control of our government services, providing an artificial security blanket over all of us — a responsibility never defined in our Constitution.

In the 1960s we, of our generation, believed that any and everything was possible, perhaps creating the idyllic "Camelot". We created cars powerful enough to generate many personal speeding tickets, and the decreasing need of personnel to produce more than we can consume. We watched our astronauts walk on the moon's surface, expanding our awed visions of space and the fragile vulnerabilities of our Earth. In contrast, because of Viet Nam, we also started to realize that we use an increasing number of weapons and physical confrontations to settle our differences, rather than use peace in creating answers.

In the mid 1960s there was a concerted effort by the private sector to teach people how to listen, to consciously understand the words being used by the person doing the talking. In essence, to mentally focus on another human being, learning another's thinking process and eventually absorb their point of view. With research and development investment of several hundred millions of dollars by corporate America, the results were implemented into the inner workings of numerous sales and marketing forces to sell production rather than to teach the general public and our politicians how to listen to each other.

The numerous studies summarized that we retain approximately 20% of what we hear if what is being said is of interest to us. The average human attention span is less than four seconds if it isn't. Likewise we, mortals, retain 50% of what is read and 95% of what is physically, emotionally and mentally experienced. If what is being discussed, let's use politics and financial budgets as an example, is of no personal interest we have the habit of not paying attention, distracted about more pressing matters at that moment. When projected on a larger scale, it also explains why we have evolved into our current world because we haven't learned to communicate and listen well.

In 1969, the average family income was $8,547 because of normal inflation and global demand for our expertise. A gallon of gas cost 35 cents. A new car's average retail $3,278, a new home, $15,525. It was a period of time where things were affordable with income and family expenses in line with the other. It also initiated the foundation when we as individuals and a nation, lost our bearings and common sense laying out the foundation of the financial strains and personal anxiety of what we are experiencing today.

In 1973, gasoline retailers did quite well and the hydrocarbon industry profits exploded, damaging the foundations of Middle America. Until that year, light crude from the Middle East was priced at $1.90 to $2.80 (U.S.) per 42-gallon barrel. In less than 8 years, under the manipulated guise that the world's oil supplies were nearing exhaustion, the price escalated to $34.00 for the same quantity of product, raising wholesale prices over 1500%. We were told that the Earth had less than a 20-year supply of product, resulting in a global nightmare of personal and corporate executive anxiety and global greed.

Our government leadership went into its typical mode of political reaction, skewing prices throughout our economy. Instead of investigative reporting examining the true cause and effect of insider manipulation, the news and our president's office created a panicked frenzy, and public paranoia. This single year unleashed economic upheaval on the global economy with America's workers having to work two jobs in order for their families to survive the ravages of inflation. It also created the United States becoming the world's largest debtor, laying the foundation of energy shortages and today's product manipulation and our current dependence on foreign oil.

All management in all companies, in all industries, then went into a financial tailspin of crises management. Profit taking was jeopardized with the rising price of product and its related transportation costs. Corporate America then began rising their wholesale pricing to offset the new cost of doing business. Prices were then increased at each service level, adding to their bottom line, with the consumer paying the inflated difference at retail.

The numbers and projections from our private sector caught up in this frenzy, and supported by our energy experts, forced all of us to change in a relatively short period of time. The cost of living for the average American was caught in an inflationary spiral rate of 13%-21% annually for nearly fifteen years. Companies and individuals invested for inflationary reasons, not for sound business management practices.

Insider motives of greed and manipulation were never exposed or the offenders penalized. The gasoline in the holding tanks value never came up in public discussion of who was profiting and why. The American family then needed two incomes to survive and to pay for their gasoline along with the spiraling costs of their other essentials.

The wife then started her professional career, creating the term "latch-key children," trying to stay ahead of the inflationary curve. Human nature being what it is then led into a new lifestyle. Many marriages ended in divorce and single parenting and dysfunctional, emotionally damaged children, with not enough hours in the day, adding to the future social program net of welfare and Medicaid and human anger.

With the investment dollar virtually guaranteed by inflation, company management devised new methods for moneymaking. Corporate America began to invest in automation and offshore labor. Unions then countered with national strikes seeking higher wages with less output, using corporate short-term profits and job loss for justification. Short-cut taking became rampant, affecting quality controls on production and the shutdown of blue-collar jobs in America. This in turn created conflict with upper management, who driven by profit and personal compensation then accelerated the exodus. This led to the political creation of NAFTA & AFTRA by our federal government in the 1990s and widening levels of income on the executive level.

People who had the financial ability during this time placed their money into certificates of deposit and real estate, conditioned to the high rate of return. The reality and aftermath: a $15,000 home became the $150,000 asset, with our banking and savings & loan institutions guaranteeing a double-digit return on investment, leading into a half trillion dollar government bailout 16-years later.

Our executive branch of government (instead of examining insider motives, tracking the oil companies shipping manifests or physically inspecting each company's holding tanks or analyzing the true reserves globally) then reacted with Congressional intervention. A series of high-cost studies were commissioned, producing a new level of energy experts, and their support systems. Their suggestions, including conservation and alternative energy development, were determined not to be cost-effective or politically palatable for the oil companies and our economy to digest. Instead of committing to long-term energy conservation programs to include long-range planning for future availability, encouraging the private sector's development of other energy alternatives such as hydrogen, solar and wind with tax incentives, our politicians threw money into new government programs for additional study to develop no long-term practical answers.

Several-hundred tax laws were amended during the 1970s and 1980s leading into government deregulation of U.S. industry and our current corporate morass. These mandates encouraged short-term profit taking and corrupted ethical thinking while giving explosive growth to our nation's lobbying industry, an industry that is now a 70 billion dollar political support system.

Companies, then with deregulation in effect, invested for additional tax write-offs, building more shopping centers, strip malls and new residential communities by financing receptive political campaigns. This, in turn created savings & loan lending practices with few regulatory guidelines. Business investment then became skewed, geared for short-term exploitation not thinking out or planning for the long-term ramifications. Labor unions then fought for income increases tied into the inflationary levels pricing U.S. labor out of the competitive world market. Union demands and management expectations required accelerated product pricing at retail, with the $3,200 car now costing more than $20,000.

Money was then invested on projected future interest income creating an artificial base for money lending and taxation, leading into an accelerated formation of "Pork Barrel Legislation" to be financed by projected national income. The end result was a transfer of huge quantities of cash from the public's wallets to corporations and the failure of our S&L's programs, costing the American taxpayer over $500,000,000,000 (five hundred billion dollars), AKA one half trillion dollars, then adding to our nation's current indebtedness.

The insiders fortunate to have deep pockets prior to this exercise profited magnificently. Companies acquired, spun-off and grew, rewarding upper corporate management and their private investment groups. The new word "junk bond" came into our vocabulary. 838,000 millionaires in 1987 grew into our current number exceeding 5,000,000 people, according to *Forbes* magazine.

The after effects of all of this are being experienced by today's families trying to keep up with the present cost of living on their credit cards in this new expensive world of ours. Home and general living overhead is no longer affordable to a shrinking Middle America with well paying jobs being downsized for corporate survival. Financial desperation has now entered the lives of most of Americans who were not in the right place at the right time.

In reflection, if OPEC members, our world's political leaders and oil conglomerates had handled a price increase wisely, this transfer would have had positive change for the world. The processes of diversifying into new energy technologies would have created new forms of environmental friendly energy development and domestic employment. Investment creating many middle-class jobs here and eventually abroad, with a safer ecology and a long-term return for the investors. Instead of our water and air being cleaner from burning less oil, or establishing a strong global middle class able to earn a livable income on a single salary, this transition produced unusual growth in the Netherlands, Cayman and Swiss bank accounts for a small handful of players. Most of us, the paying market on a global scale, are now unable to financially get ahead of the curve of our present costs of survival.

The tempo of the human-stress level is spiraling with this new cost for survival. The outcome is now demanding a hefty price and a heavy mental toll. We are now in a frustrated combat mode, attempting to survive the financial and human demands of each day's growing pressures. The human pace is escalating as seen in the eyes of each driver speeding on our interstate highway systems filled with stress and increasing instances of road rage; or the tears of a parent who has just lost a child to drugs and gang warfare.

There are now too many uneducated people living around us ill-prepared for the challenges of living in our current world, who can be easily manipulated. We are a generation faced with declining opportunities with climbing responsibilities — a group finding ourselves in an involuntary free fall. We are also a generation that has just received a major wake-up call.

We have evolved into a society reliant upon massive government intervention in our personal lives, with law making displacing the responsibilities of a self-reliant individual and family unit. Bureaucratic growth and spending on government programs have become the rule of the day with our governments role never defined or outlined in our Bill of Rights or Constitution. Medicaid, Medicare, unemployment, food and housing subsidies introduced to address human need and managed by a burgeoning governmental bureaucracy are fulfilling roles that were never planned for, or prescribed, as our Nation's governing responsibilities.

Our world today has been artificially sped up and "bastardized" with hidden agenda decisions, and the mistake making of our politicians far removed from the realities of us the country's common citizens. Political decisions are coming faster and faster with all levels of government intervention escalating, the complexity in our lives increasing and the future expense, both human and financial a big unknown. We are also being shown that we do not pay attention to our history well. This past is now being replicated and personally experienced at this writing, 30 years after this sting on all of World.

****

On the morning of September 11, over 100 million Americans awakened, many sleep- deprived, showered, probably ate breakfast, then went to work or began the first day of their vacation. A few of this number gave their children a hug, petted their pet, kissed their spouse or significant other, wished them a great day, before leaving their homes. Each person was probably thinking about the day's schedule with advancing financial and time pressures on the shoulders of many, none thinking of a looming disaster. Around 9:00 that same morning almost 2,900 human souls were dramatically removed from this world. Not one of this number, or their surviving families, knew that they were going to die that day.

We, the surviving audience, were psychologically and spiritually etched that moment, subconsciously marked with the reality that the unthinkable happened. The security and personal freedoms we took for granted all of our lives were breeched in just a few moments of visual impact. The immediate aftermath on our conscious minds was an innermost feeling of an emptiness and vulnerable concern. Most, if not all of us, became temporarily alone, seeking answers to the question, why?

We, and our nation, are now comparable to the child adolescent growing into adulthood with comparable fits and starts. We are able to reach the stars, and place men on the moon and surround our planet with thousands of satellites. We have the ability to move information globally at blinding speed and will come to the aid of most nations in their time of need. We live in a country that is capable of influencing the rest of the world with our experiences, wealth and strength. We have a consistent history of overcoming most adversity against all odds. But never in all of recorded time has a civilization come so far, so fast, and been so challenged mentally and spiritually. We are learning that each day is given to us as a loan, not more.

We now reside in a world, divided, based on the gross manipulations of a handful of powerful people, with incivility and human despair running rampant, globally. These persons, like many of us, have a tendency to get caught up in their own importance and personal ineptitude leading into their decision making and greed, not comprehending the human toll and the larger alternatives. Their agendas are driven by politics, money and power and their personal lack of civility and compassion for human life. Terrorism, regional warfare, human despair and widening divisions in wealth are now the result, and are common threads of our many past diversions.

Dependent upon where one is in this spiritual journey of ours, with our various interpretations of life and death, we can envision that these 2,900 souls were volunteered as our secular wake-up call on the 11th. Or we can realize by secularized measurements that the walls of our personal indifference and ignorance to the plight of the rest of the world are now surfacing on our domestic shores. We are now entering into the self-recognition phase of realizing what we have become. Children, untethered from our Father's original intentions for us, running dangerously out of control.

We now have the choice of using our free will to decide which way we will travel for the rest of our lifetimes. Either we can move to a higher plane of understanding, addressing our past errors, improving our existence from what we will do; or we can keep on hoping that God will somehow intervene to keep us from destroying ourselves. There are no guarantees today, as in the past, that this will be the outcome.

We have a modern history of being pretty arrogant, ignoring the many messages of our times. Out of this equation each of us can be brought to the realization that our existence on this planet is a fragile, tenuous enterprise. Our capacity to listen to our surroundings will eventually govern which direction we choose. The Earth's problems are globally massive and extremely deadly. And we have created a world of short attention spans, not able to listen to ourselves.

Instead of intuitively hearing what nature and our situations are telling us, we respond with more industrial and personal pollution with growing landfills and political negativity. Our coral reefs and sea life (like the caged canary in a coal mine is a harbinger of a natural gas leak) are turning a dull cancerous gray, transformed by our surface activity. Sunlight in many of our world's cities is now filtered through yellowish-brown atmospheres, thickened by the oxides of our creation. Because of our secular decisions and a lack of political vision, we now have human genocide and mass starvation in many parts of the world, while the First World has a problem of obesity. The outcomes are now our waste and growing military expense, requiring our nation's policing of the World, enforced by our armed services. It is a fragile coexistence in a world held together with bubble gum, fear, rhetorical smoke and mirrors, nearing a moral and financial bankruptcy.

Our unique experiment of governing democratically is now challenged to move into a new chapter, establishing higher priorities and methods of thinking, to awaken as God's children. And to start listening to that little voice inside each one of us, then do something constructive with what is being said. Or we can continue this path and like all others, Rome, Greece etc. fail from within. We are now receiving daily reports that we are all on the receiving end, with acid rain, breaks in the ozone and living in an increasing dangerous world splintered by these realities and division. Millions of persons, who want the same as you or me, are continually dying at the hands of some very sick people driven by their individual perceptions of their world, resenting us for what we are trying to do.

It is for all of these reasons, and many more too numerous to mention, that our modern lives are now teetering on the edge of a physical implosion. A period where our inner souls are seeking some form of sanity and hope in a world that is going insane. The following are but a few suggestions to introduce future thinking and hopefully open a discussion leading into voluntarily planned change. To realize that when we become truly silent and listen within ourselves, each one of us will develop our own conclusions and eventual truth.

From this time on, if we elect to listen to the negative events in each of our lives, we can sense that we are becoming charged to do things differently, to hear what our conscious minds and hearts and souls are telling us. To think about what is going on around us, becoming more sensitive and compassionate as individuals, realizing what we have evolved into.
Perhaps, in this comprehend the words "cause" and "effect" to take prudent care of our neighbors and the Earth for the rest of our lifetimes. And to listen to all of the messages around us, developing compassionate answers for our great-grandchildren's tomorrows. Their lives, and all of the lives of our following generations, are dependent on what we do today.

CHAPTER X
SPIRITUALITY

Finding God is a complex, most personal journey. An electrical ether and grand scientist motivated by pure unconditional love is hard to embrace conceptually, making this existence most difficult to humanly comprehend. God is an intuitive travel so intricate and individually intense, that wars have been fought, lives thrown in turmoil and ideologies sacrificed, seeking a personal solace in this absolute perfection. His universe, not ours, is infinite in its majesty and symmetrical balance, with no time restraints. Jesus was placed on this Earth to explain God's purpose for us and to act as a conduit to our Creators loving grace. Two thousand years later, we still do not grasp the simplicity of this message.

The Milky Way Galaxy, which sustains this planet's travel, is one of over one billion galaxies, suspected to the third power, ad-infinitum, by the findings of the Hubble Telescope and our scientific world. Each galaxy is made up of approximately 400 billion suns, themselves surrounded by a larger number of planets. All are encompassed by a newfound dark energy, which surrounds all matter. It can be reasoned from this description, that who or whatever created this Earth and all of its living creatures is far beyond what we are able to comprehend with our mortal minds. Only with this humbling written perspective, can we sense that we have been very blessed to be alive in human form, existing on this self-contained spaceship, Earth.

Whether one leans towards the concept of Darwin's linear explanation of evolution or Divine intervention of a higher power's hand, each of us can appreciate that what we were originally given was well thought out and didn't happen by accident. Through our life experiences, our mutual trials and tribulations and errors, we can recognize this creation as a common denominator of all of mankind, producing the sameness of our human souls.

Over the years in my travels, I have experienced the many beautiful areas of this Earth, and some of the "ugliest" places filled with ecological chaos and human tragedy. Through this, I am now sharing a different perspective generated by the messages left on me through these journeys. Memories well scorched into my mind and inner soul, the result of my lifetime spent in these two different worlds.

During these trips for both business and pleasure, I was fortunate to have met a handful of persons with the capacity to communicate with not just their voice, but with an intuitive depth rarely understood by many of us. What I mean, in explanation, is that we were able to discuss global and national events with not just our mouths and ears but through the intricate workings of our internal souls. Although strangers temporarily traveling together we were able relate to, then sense, the joys, frustrations and setbacks that we had in our lives with a compassionate, deeper understanding. In essence, we were kindred spirits communicating with each other through the grace of our Father, far beyond what any of us are formally taught to do in our schools.

Maybe this has happened to you at one time or another in your life. You meet someone for the first time, yet it seems as if you have known each other for a lifetime through a quick heart felt connect. In this, you are able to feel and cover encyclopedias of knowledge beyond what your mind would normally interpret; far beyond a superficial contact that many of us have with each other. The terminology "kindred soul" comes to mind and I will leave it at that.

Looking back it was a blessing produced at that time to have us learn something for later use. Those past brief moments of human contact are presently guiding these words being used. I do not want to get off track or confuse you in this thought, nor do I want you to form a quick emotional judgment closing off this communication. It is this type of thought-transference, that has the potential to have us start looking at and doing things differently as human beings. Mahatma Gandhi, Einstein and Jules Verne were initially scoffed at for their larger thinking as examples, but what they projected then produced what is now part of today's society.

Today as I digest this in reflection, I realize that we do not know how to use the larger internal human communication systems our Father has provided. We do not listen well internally to what is being said by our surroundings to us and to each other. To date we have a hard enough time dealing with what we have which has created this world around us, let alone to think about going into a different communication level for future human development and compassionate understanding. Yet, I know from these words being produced, that we have the ability to communicate with each other on deeper spiritual levels, bridging our human differences when we open ourselves in allowing this to happen.

Because of our lack of education and inexperience in this area we have been conditioned to think on finite, not infinite terms in closed boxes of time reference, limiting ourselves as a human body. Through this we are molded, then handicapped by our perceptions, formed and reinforced by all of the secular events that enter and then emotionally control our lives. We ebb and flow in our intuitive spiritual development from this, causing our various religious interpretations (i.e. Catholic, Baptist, Hindu and Moslem etc.), keeping us separated from each other and our Father.

Perhaps through this thought process, we can reach out to each other overcoming our current perceptions and past mistakes; then address our many growing problems with plausible answers, planning out our mutual tomorrows allowing God's will, and not ours to be done.

****

Many of us can relate to the love of a parent willing to sacrifice to allow a child to survive and grow in a productive manner. A guiding hand to avoid a negative outcome. An adult always on call to lend advice, assisting the young person to mature; a parental protection of warmth and loving concern which provides a sound foundation for that child, as he grows older. An adult who will allow each child to learn from his or her mistakes, keeping them from harm's way while growing intuitively. This is what our Father is truly all about, not to make our lives difficult, but to provide the parental direction through His unconditional love.

When all else fails and we reach a point of breaking, we oftentimes pray and allow the time to listen to that little voice inside of us. Through this, we find an inner sanctum to ask for a quick fix to our problems; or to find an inner comfort, then a warm response to a specific need at a specific moment.

When we process this interaction with our conscious minds, we sense a small internal response. With our soul then connecting to our brain, we feel a form of energy surrounded by a calming peace and sense of order. Once this level of communication is obtained, when we allow our mind to flow freely, minimizing our conscious mental activity to not interfere with the moment. As this happens our thoughts, our fears and concerns are moved to the forefront of the conversation, sensing that God is listening with you. It maybe just a brief contact for that moment or a continuation forevermore; as we have the gift of free will and free choice. This path is allowed to us every day of our lives to strengthen our belief systems in Him, as His children. All that happens good and bad; all that we that we consciously do in dealing with the day's pressures and human demands, translates into a spiritual molding process provided by our Creator. Every moment we receive is provided as a private learning curve to keep our souls and us balanced.

In seeking the answers to why our lives are becoming so difficult and dangerous, supposedly protected by our God, clear religious explanations are muddled by our need for manmade boxes and the agendas of organized religion with its separating doctrines. We do not look into ourselves with a binding and instinctive understanding. We have forgotten that we are here to remember our mutual beginnings, nothing more or less.

Because of our lack in understanding this, we now have over 19,000 denominations in the world, each believing that their interpretations are correct. This frays what we intuitively sense, distorted by half-truths.

Since the times of recorded history the victors of any battle manipulate the actual events to advance their cause. The survivors and their scribes of all of recorded time have produced the writings we base our religious beliefs and current interpretations upon, keeping us globally divided and confrontational. These historical renderings are to sometimes educate, but more often their purpose is to sedate, then control the masses into submissions to authority. The dogmas of our many religions, devised by secularized agendas have created our many deadly human divisions, taking what should be so simple, making it a most complicated journey.

Most religions, worldwide, worship the one same Creator, but many are heatedly divided to the point of creating human hatred in their doctrines. These secularized positions do not embrace God's purpose and His original intentions for all humankind.

Not wanting us to be automatons, our Father gave us free will, the ability to consistently make our own decisions with His guiding hand. Out of this, we are given continual choices of creating a dependence on a higher belief; then growing consciously and mentally, or ignoring it totally.

Through the events of our times, we are now rediscovering that the future of our spiritual evolution is dependent on our moving on past this conditioning, with each of us coming together as a family of equals in God's vision. Each of us is sharing this path of a continual journey. All of us are mutually being challenged to grow into a higher awareness, learning then responding to the many lessons now being heard.

Religion and spirituality are individual concepts dependent upon one's personal life experiences and education in coping with the hand we are dealt. There are those who believe that our existence is a continual spiritual journey growing with our efforts and presence, learning from our experiences, moving on to a different plane of development. Our souls move from era to era learning or remembering a lesson we voluntarily chose before our births. And when the time is right, the experience learned, that soul moves on to continue the process after our mortal death.

There are others who with all their hearts, minds and souls believe in a definite Heaven and Hell filled with demons. What one does during one's lifetime will determine where that soul will end up for all Eternity. Hopefully, moving on to Heaven for doing good deeds for their families and friends and worshiping God while living on this Earth.

They believe that we have but one life to live and we better do it well, as there is a future price that will be paid. Then, there are a small number who deny the existence of God altogether, and lean to believing that all things are influenced by the nature of things as outline by Darwin. That when we die we return to dust; that this life we are presently living is all that there is. These various interpretations continue into the tens of thousands, worldwide, creating a maze of needless complexity and human division and despair, taking our Father's existence, splintering His intention, making His simple love so needlessly complex.

God has a unique method of communicating personally with each one of us in His attempt to keep us voluntarily on track, as previously mentioned. It is the warming sensation we feel in our hearts and the throb in the middle of our chest connected to the sensors of our minds never explained in any dictionary, Bible or medical journal that we have on this Earth. This inner sense keeps us on a positive course for our emotional well being, adding to our spiritual depth appreciating God's underlying love.

All of us have been on the receiving end of some unexplained event or a person coming into our lives with an answer to a specific problem. It may be a solution to a serious event we created or through the efforts of others, or a child just reaching out to give us a hug at the right time, bringing a smile and a tear, to our eyes. Each of these unexpected moments, all of the good and bad things that enter our lives, are a continual series of lessons with our beings softly molded to recognize the spirits we are. We should embrace the fact that our current existence is a series of these journeys and jolts, the aftereffects a payment in kind.

Our secular motivations with their hidden agendas, and our human pride cause us to lose sight of His originating intentions as our loving Parent. With God's blessing of our free wills, when we listen from within, we have the option to choose, in this case to turn our tragedies and the loss of American lives on September 11th into a better world. We also have the choice of ignoring this voice from within, eventually forgetting the impact of this direct message.

It is our current challenge to choose via our "free will" which path we will take that will affect our children's lifetimes, breaking the back of our histories repeating themselves. God supplies each of us with our miracles and a moral survival code. Bombarded by so much cruelty and needless death, we can become quite cynical and helpless, but instead we will take the Golden Rule seriously, addressing the problems of those in need, attempting to balance off the damages created from within.

Sometimes we move forward in a positive progression of our evolution and maturity when the message of a loving parent is listened to and followed, and oftentimes backward with us never quite wanting to hear, or follow what is being said. Each of us is on this same journey of remembering who and what we are as a child of God to become prudent in surviving the hand that mortal life has dealt us. Our overall purpose is to realize that we are charged to spend our time while on this Earth, as His children, seeking avenues for a peaceful coexistence, improving the conditions on this Earth. And to eventually overcome our cultural differences in coping with a dysfunctional family system.

When we take the time to subconsciously listen to the sounds within each of us, we use our intuitive imaginations. In total silence, we are able to envision the gurgling of an early environment, the nutrients of life being passed through the umbilical before we are born. Soothing sounds of the crashing volume waves make when hitting the Earth, its millions of bubbles bursting on impact with the sand on the shore and in our subconscious minds. When we are able to truly listen from within, we sense an internal peace in our mind and our soul. We feel in total harmony with the universe.

All of us, on many different levels, are innately overwhelmed with the creation of another being as a personal blessing from God. It is an innocent period of provision that includes a parent's love, comforted and being comforted, and for a newborn, eventually receiving a clean diaper. We can also envision the titanic forces it took to have the fetus leave what was most comfortable and secure, head first into an unknown world with eyes held tightly closed. Then opened out of curiosity.

We, in this generation, are being asked to open our eyes, as all generations past, to create this common thread similar to the intuitive feelings of a new born baby — eventually leading into an initial blueprint of our future regeneration. Then to open a verbal debate and thought process of personally and spiritually listening to what God has said to us in our past, and what he is saying to us now. Out of this we can add simplicity to our lives, building a sense of purpose and unity, overcoming our current disastrous man made odds.

We have the option to slow things down into a digestible format, to truly listen to all that is being said when we open ourselves in allowing this to happen. We have been lovingly warned, many times, about what we were doing through the many vehicles that God uses — fact and truth. Yet, instead of doing the responsible right things, using our intuitions and common sense in addressing our ills, we create human walls of our political and sometimes personal belligerence, ignoring the much larger message. Global warming, holes in our ozone, localized terrorism, death and distortion to many life species, destructions of the Earth's forest, contaminated air, water and lands, HIV and AIDS are all of His messages being ignored.

God has been telling us, as a very concerned parent, that we are now auctioning off all of our future life support systems to support our immediate travels. All combined have the real potential to create a perilous and deadly journey for our children and all following generations. We are now being consciously awakened through all that is happening around us, including the events inspired by bin Laden and company, to allow our inner awareness to surface addressing what we have allowed to be created, to start thinking on a higher plane of reference as to who we are, the responsibilities we have, understanding what we will eventually become.

He knows, far better than we, that our global and personal mistakes and pains are now so excessive that extreme measures are being allowed to use current events as our wake-up call to start paying attention to this world of His. It will be through God's assistance and our visualization by faith that will provide the avenues to survive our modern-day pressures, to stay whole and sane. The key is to start listening to the world surrounding us as the children of God — something we stopped doing too long ago.

In moving forward, with what will be suggested in this book, I ask you to not only pray but also discuss your concerns, your hopes and dreams and personal setbacks and fears with God, and to become tolerant and forgiving of our past errors as we are all carrying very heavy baggage.

Ask about what you have interpreted to this point and ask for the belief, faith and time to become involved by opening yourself to listen to God's response and forgiveness. Pray for a conscious direction, allowing our Father's will to be done to possibly utilize you as a vehicle to institute a positive change in our current world. And to release all of your pent up hatreds and fears believing that this will be a new day.

Structure your thoughts with a linear approach of definition, in secular terms, allowing yourself to be opened to change. To truly understand that without our Creator's involvement in this process that you, and we, are in real trouble as the magnitude of what has to be accomplished is beyond our human ability to play the current game of life.

He, as our singular and multiple parent, only wants the best for us and as a loving parent will provide a guiding and protecting hand when asked. And like any loving parent, when He sees a child about to do something that has the potential to do harm, He will warn each child of the danger.

Since in His world there is no beginning, or end, or pain, He continually looks over us, allowing our human checks and balances and our free wills to prevail, which is part of the umbrella He provides. For, many reasons we will never fathom as mortals, God has a way of taking care of His fools and children in these travels continually confirming His existence and concern.

On September the 11, 2001, His guiding hand filled with patience, love and grace protected us. Instead of the Twin Trade Towers imploding from within, dropping straight down, a domino effect could have cascaded down the center of Manhattan, or a nuclear reactor plant hit killing millions of Americans. Although difficult for us to understand, we were sheltered that day from what could have been a far worse disaster, the timing and a perfect response to our specific need, at the proper moment.

Rather than finding fault with Him for allowing this tragedy to happen, we should find fault in us for providing the nucleus of this devastation. Each day we are surrounded with news of tremendous ecological destructions, tornadoes, earthquakes and fires which do tremendous carnage to our physical structures, yet there is little loss of human life because of His patience with us and His unconditional love.

In moving forward, it will be imperative to discern that if anyone or anything is harmed or one profits at the expense to others by what we will eventually do, then what is being heard is wrong. If any remodeling or program has the potential to place devastation, or heartbreak in our lives the messages received are not initiated by God. For this reason, the balance of these words and ideas being shared will need to be placed in prayerful thought for you to personally determine if they are correct.

Plato, a most insightful person 3,000 years ago, came to the conclusion that a good society produces good people. And good people act nobly and care, learning from their mutual successes and failures, to cooperate in peace with each other. This same philosophy and thinking prevails today in addressing our moral breakdowns and listening with our inner sanctums. Through this acceptance our life experiences and ingenuity can move the proverbial mountain, which is something we are now faced with.

Over ninety percent of us in this country say we believe in God, which could support a moral and prudent redirection for our country, and eventually the rest of the world. If this number is acceptable to you, our religious leaders can recognize that they and we are not living with the faith that comes with this belief.

Living should be a simple interplay between man and nature with a personal sensitivity, an inner awareness of His presence and loving kindness. Each of us accepting the fact that we have been truly blessed to be alive with our human existence provided by a loving Father who, in His loving-kindness, also created Darwin.

Our religious bodies lost their spiritual focus and our nation's moral direction, when they didn't pray for God's intercession during our secular transitions of the 1960s. By allowing our government and judicial processes to enter into the arena of interpreting, then governing societal mores, our religious institutions relinquished their reason for existence, as the bride of Christ.

History has continually shown that when the spiritual body loses sight of its originating purpose the social outcomes are the repetitions of wars, famines, plagues, revolutions, flooding, false religious leanings with religious deceptions and political disasters. Today our headlines are filled with this insaneness, mirroring the duplication of organized religion's history with this transference. Mass shootings, regional wars, human genocide, children disrespecting their parents and killing each other, then committing suicide, our moral infrastructure and fiber has broken down. Disproportionate income for services rendered in the corporate and sports worlds, embezzlement of investors funds, mega-mergers failing in huge numbers, ecological disasters intensifying — and the list goes on.

Rather than bringing us together as God's children, addressing our many dysfunctions, our many organized religious institutions now find themselves in direct competition, floundering with each other, waiting for God's supreme intervention. Most seek secular solutions addressing the many symptoms, not addressing the original cause. As God initially provided Nature with Her own internal checks and balances, we also share the same set of dynamics in our internal awareness for repair. Today, because of our escalating difficulties, our spiritual barometers on all levels are being consciously raised to embrace the fact that the time is now to evolve to a higher purpose.

The morning of September 11th provided us with that window for an intuitive understanding of the much larger picture. To slow down and to think about what we are doing to ourselves. To start listening to the many messages we are now beginning to hear. Then do something positive with what is being heard. And to develop a larger spiritual bonding between us as human beings, with all of us eventually communicating through a much deeper level of human understanding.

Each of our communities has religious organizations and volunteers that help us become more civil and compassionate to each other, creating a less hostile world. There are many support groups reaching out to address our many serious illnesses and local needs. Our news is filled with persons who for some unexplainable reason enter the lives of others to aid in a time of need nationally, globally and locally, as evidenced by the events following the morning of the 11th. Our current generational task is to grasp the dynamics of these many sides of this equation, discerning the results of the decisions of others, and the universal impact it has had on each one of us.

CHAPTER XI
HUMAN VALUES

When we are born into this world we have a childlike innocence with no boxed in mentality, or human prejudice. We, perhaps, are simply looking forward to experiencing the life in front of us. In this, we do not really pay attention to who is lying next to us, probably more distracted by the wonderments surrounding our little bodies. Maybe we are just thankful to be alive, healthy and hope to be loved for our lifetimes.

We find out very early in the nurturing process that if our diaper is soiled or we are hungry we will use any method available to us to get our parents' attention to fix our personal problems. Through this we learn to push certain emotional buttons to gain a favorable response. If smiling doesn't work, we will then produce a temper tantrum, howling in our misery, gaining we hope, our parents' attention to service our immediate discomfort.

When two adults marry and decide to have children it is a lifetime commitment, with both persons working together to nurture the lives of their offspring. In this process, parents will try to make things easier for the newborns, applying what they previously learned from their lessons in life. They will sacrifice almost anything to keep a child from making a mistake, or to keep that child out of harm's way. On the larger scale, we mirror this same human response as we have now secured the full attention of God who, like a natural parent, is trying to protect His children from damaging themselves.

Our world's psychological and social experts are now finding that the first three years of our childhood and the first three years of our education lay the foundations of who and what we will be as adults. That when we as children are nurtured with love, compassion and intelligence, we will with few exceptions emulate the process, as we grow older.

In this, they recognize that almost 70% of our moral upbringing and our attitudes toward others are initiated through family interaction and the pressure of our peers. That if our natural parents love each other and are able to supply a newborn's basic life necessities, that each child brought into this world has the early foundations to simply smile as an adult. Contrastingly, these same studies find that when a child is mentally and emotionally abused, these factors then lay the foundations to be replicated in adult behavior. That if a child is not loved or wanted, or their parents ignore the root cause of their emotional behavior; this baggage, with few exceptions, will be carried for life, bringing consistent pain.

History has shown that when one generation cares deeply about the responsibilities that come from living life, that this concern is passed on to its following generations. With all the above it would be safe to conclude (with a little mental stretch) that when our youth are shown that their lives are worth living, that the "grown-up" world is aware of its responsibilities and is doing something intelligent to sensitively address them, would instill a hope for a better future. (This would also have an immediate effect on their and our current human behavior, my opinion).

Conversely, if we are in a world guided by adults who show little interest with the responsibilities of parenting, we oftentimes end up with a following generation becoming more abusive and shortsighted. That when a leader of a business corporation or country is exposed to an unloved early existence, conditioned to lie, cheat, steal and use physical force in response to a perceived challenge, this conditioning will normally surface as an adult. This correlation (if we are inclined to look at the early lives of the current world's business despots and world dictators), would allow us to reason to be the "cause and effect" of most wars, domestic terrorism and corruptive business abuse in our man-made global world.

From this it is safe to believe that we have these two options. Either we carefully embrace the responsibilities of parenting in a prudent loving manner showing our children that we care; or we can keep on doing what we are doing in nurturing a dismal future for our nation's offspring.

We should be thankful that we live in this country. All one has to do is experience what other people and countries don't have and the circumstances they are attempting to survive. For whatever reason, maybe the luck of the draw, we reside in the greatest country on this planet. We share an existence filled with a history of being an innovative group, willing to experiment, oftentimes overcoming monstrous odds.

Most of us were raised in a moral society to have the perception that there was a semblance of sense and sanity in our lives. As we matured we began to learn that there were many forms of constructive order and destructive chaos as any generation experiences, but there seemed to be a positive light at the end of the tunnel for the majority. Because of a slower moving world then, with less artificial distractions, it was a period more in harmony with our internal energies and the inner workings of this planet.

Through our nation's visionaries we were able to place men on the moon using our human ingenuity and daring, in less than a decade from its initiation. We were able to harness the energy of the atom; invent the computer with its internal, "infernal" driving software. And now we are in the throes of manipulating our DNA for "supposed" health reasons. Through this we are venturing into the unknown. We are also learning that we do not have all of the answers and can be blindsided so quickly. Events of our times are new in their unprecedented scope because our current dysfunctions are being piloted by our misguided perceptions.

With any steps forward, there are many steps backwards with the many lessons learned. The future is evolving from what we presently do. Our external driving mechanisms are now teaching us to think and feel differently, to become more aware to the needs of this world. What transpired on the morning of the 11th was unimaginable to many of us until that day. The impact of those few televised moments became the imaginable forevermore. These brief months following those four collisions are a forewarning that if we keep on doing what we have been doing we will be in deeper trouble than we are currently.

At this writing we are on a war footing in the Middle East, and are being publically threatened by one of our Asian neighbors (possessing nuclear weapons), and are about to force our Nations' will on the rest of the world. These situations and our escalating times are challenging us to contemplate and creatively ingest were we are going as a free society, under God in this madness. We are learning that we are very vulnerable to the many pressure of this world, now in the real danger of losing what we have gained too easily.

Most of us today are being distracted from the real issues by disinformation and in a race to cram as much as we can into a twenty-four hour time period, while trying to keep our heads above water and ahead of our creditors. Increasing numbers of us are now attempting to cope with an accelerating world and the fallout of these transitions. We have not been taught to digest the human cost of this escalation, with many of us now experiencing personal and emotional turmoil nearing the point of mental burnout.

Today everything we think we possess, our health, money, every family member, adult, child and friend in each of our lives, is most fragile and on a temporary loan. Each of us in our own individual way is in the process of being taught to become humble, by the escalating events of these times. To recognize that this Earth and all we have does not belong to man, as all that we see, feel, touch and breathe belongs to the graciousness of God.

We have the hard challenge of acknowledging our past errors and confronting the future with new governing formats built on trust, altering the depths of our education to overcome our present mental conditioning. We are a nomadic people, who when we become displeased with our concreted existence and waste, have a history of creating new paths to pursue a better outcome. By thinking on larger, more benevolent terms we together can formulate the foundations of new thought, by listening internally to that conscious voice inside each one of us.

In this we will find that each one of us can share our talents and experience, leading the rest of the world by internal example and our enterprise. We can emerge into a functioning global unit, with each person, worldwide, eventually becoming responsible for creating his own destiny. We are a nation made up of diverse ethnic strengths with many divergent interests. We are a compassionate nation built on a moral heritage with numerous collective assets. This has the real potential of providing the nucleus to create the base for our future, learning from our recent histories and building on our national strengths.

We will have the capacity to improve the quality of life when our government leaders and corporate America understand they also have the evolved human responsibilities of being good parents for their personal children. The initial goal and eventual outcome is to have each of us on all socioeconomic levels, become motivated by our basic human traits, leading into a more sensitive, spiritual awareness producing an national alteration.

We are a society in desperate need of corporate morals and civility tied in with common sense values, and a road map to let us know where our leadership is taking us. To not create divisions of philosophy and wealth strategies through partisan politics and corruptive greed, but to bring us together with our Father and neighbor with vision and compassion for our fellow man. Through media coverage, talking and listening with our souls, we can eventually be educated to do things differently, engineering a positive future for our children and eventually ourselves in this evolution.

Future programming can incorporate our many personal issues and capabilities to eventually permeate each family unit. In this, each of us can learn to become responsible for our personal health, education and welfare, and to establish a solid foundation to build upon. To create a private enterprise of educating our children on a global basis, while eliminating the corruption of politics, and the inefficiencies permeating education's mismanagement.

We are in an era where we are strongly motivated by money and what we see, we will therefore need a short-term goal of creating worldwide employment, restoring this earth using our subconscious imaginations. Incorporating a sweat-equity mentality while paying livable incomes that will establish human self-worth and a better world. Through this, we will be able to address the many social and ecological problems we share by making our decisions democratically.

This will be a major, but small part, of the overall equation being presented. Out of this we can initiate the foundation of a future existence, eventually becoming less dependent on government intervention motivated by the dollar. The key is to tie in all the above while simultaneously addressing the environmental disasters we have in this overpopulated, chaotic world. Because if we lose this spaceship and Her support systems all else will be but a moot point

Benevolent future change is going to require that we become more self-reliant and less dependent upon our government's social interventions and its corruptive inefficiencies. The world's economists will eventually need to embrace the cash-flow apparatus to think out profit taking in the long-term, with the business community becoming less dependent on consumer consumption. Then to think out a national, then global, corporate plan addressing the roles of government and our collective social responsibilities. A future goal managed by our following generations motivated by peace, compatibility and unconditional love.

****

Our forefathers, Franklin, Jefferson, Washington and most of their generation, were conditioned to hear as children, listening to their inner selves to overcome adverse conditions. They recognized, or were led to internally believe, that we are all on this Earth for the purpose of improving what we inherit. By looking at all of their alternatives they were able to turn a bad situation into an opportunity leading us into a democracy.

Through God's influence and their need to personally survive over oppression, our society, through their inspirations, received a moral written code providing for the freedoms we have. Over a period of several years and numerous written drafts, they were able to address the main problems of human divisions with a self-governing format incorporating common sense, directives. Their efforts and inspirations provided an outline for future generations by following their faith, human instinct and innermost thoughts.

Through their listening prowess, a final formulation of all four of these motivators produced a Declaration of Independence breaking away from England; and eventually drafting our Constitution and Bill of Rights, providing not only hope, but new thinking.

By conceptualizing our current events in broader terms, absorbing all the knowledge we have in a digestible format, we can become instrumental in creating a 21st Century which will not only eventually benefit our children's children but each one of us, and in turn all others. An effort that is going to take the energies and stretch the abilities of all factions having diverse agendas to create a course for human change and reverse our history's negative repetitions.

Our challenges today are so diverse, so convoluted and personal that without God in our equation we will never be able to address our many challenges in a compassionate and prudent manner. Spiritual, political and corporate leaders, and we ourselves, will eventually need to open each of our souls, and learn as a mass audience to concentrate on our human sameness and not our political and cultural differences.

All of us can become dependent practitioners on listening with our intuitions and compiling our current data to recognize what was and is still working collectively for the betterment of man. As a common denominator, we should eventually be able to realize that even with all the differences we have with all the others around us, we share many of the same concerns and human objectives. The person living in poverty has the same human need as those living in the ivory towers of the corporate world, to love and be loved and have a sense of security. And to have a roof over their heads with food on their tables, to believe that each of us is part of some larger answer to some type of harmonious mosaic we don't quite, or will ever understand.

When we learn to understand our sameness in all of our needs as humankind, we can provide the moral guidance to incorporate the knowledge we possess in this modern age of technology. In this we can visualize, then implement, a major re-engineering of our nation comparable to the Marshall Plan and the United Nations combined. Eventually reversing the damage of war, greed and our human ignorance. In essence, compiling all that we have at our fingertips, creating a modern day Alexandria using the United States as a base for trial and error, for eventual global implementation.

In this we can use our life experiences on a local and national level and utilize patience in most, if not all, that we do; while implanting the words civility, compassion and empathy into what we will eventually become. Then allow persons who are able to remain calm under adversity and to look at things in the philosophical long-term, to become instrumental in having their natural gifts surface.

We can look at things with a broader perspective and project the ramifications of long-term "effect" on our decision-making processes. With this we can embrace our differences of race, culture and diverse opinions, developing the pieces we have as a nation and put the puzzle together. And to have each of us become personally concerned about the condition of this world, that all of us will someday leave. As said several times earlier, if we destroy our Earth because of our noninvolvement and the way we currently do things, all else we will ever think or do or feel will end up becoming nothing but a myth and a long lost memory.

All of us are born with natural gifts — mental, physical and spiritual, which if consciously developed, could carry each of us a very long way in accommodating future change. Each of us knows of someone who, somehow or other, is able to take the most complex of things and explain it in a simple manner; it may be an instructor in the classroom teaching Algebra, Geometry or the English language who is able to create that "light bulb" effect, where others fail, or a parent successfully discussing the continuation of life after death to a child filled with fear. There are individuals involved in business and social programs who through their personal concerns and teaching effort are able to institute a positive change, taking what is not working and transforming it into something positive.

There are individuals who have the special gift of vision and healing, the ability of digesting past and current facts, initiating a corporate overview and putting the pieces together, who have the potential of developing a master concept with a plan. There are a multitude of visionaries who are able to picture the pressing questions that must be asked, utilizing common sense in creating positive, common sense law with practical applications.

It is special to be able to think in a logical manner and communicate with others with not just the ears and voice, but also with the heart and one's mind. The lesson is to listen with our souls twice as much as we talk, comprehending the words being used. Persons who understand this and discuss problems with thoughtful remedies will be our future social architects developing change. When a person or a group of people is shown that they are special, reinforced with love in the home, school and our out-bound society, those persons will end up having a high level of self-esteem; conditioned to care for themselves and other people.

With a high energy level, intellect tied in with our ability to reason, the media and our religious institutions would be able to implement compassionate change. With thought given to why things are as they are, how our present situation was created, we will be able to grasp the cause and effect of our graphic circumstances while developing acceptable answers to our problems together.

Our future existence of either peace or a horror show will be determined by what we do with this knowledge for lasting transformations. And how we eventually interweave our various global and local pieces together. The Earth's problems today are so massive they defy political maneuvers and partisan politics; they can't be bought or legislated away. Our personal challenge will be to overcome the mindset of just looking out for "number one" at the expense of the "community at large".

In moving forward we can democratically consider what is best for us as a nation and come to the aid of our planet as a benevolent but firm, moral world leader. We can create common-bond thinking to educate ourselves with technical learning tools and sweat equity involvement. To take the human spirit of the common man and put him back in the decision-making equation once again. We can eventually learn to discipline ourselves to take responsibility and not react in a destructive manner; in essence, get our own house in order before we find weakness in others. We can also grow into the realization that what we do individually today creates the actual history of our collective tomorrows.

If you are secure, know who you are and what your purpose is in life, you can accept these thoughts and my awkward presentation to date with an open mind. You may not agree with my thinking, but I trust you can respect my concern and approach. Through this we, together, can develop a different perspective that you may give some thought to. Out of all of this, one way or another, we will have to decide if we want others to make our decisions for us, with us paying the escalating bill. Or, if we would do a better job personally, planning our lives out for ourselves.

When I started writing the balance of this book, I found the need to create a different path for explanation. This is what I came up with. Let's see how you feel about the remaking of the United States.

CHAPTER XII
TRANSITIONS & DETAILS

On August 6, 1945 the tragic aftermath of the 11th was experienced but on a differing, more horrendous and devastating scale. The United States dropped an atomic bomb on Hiroshima. Three days later, this genocide was duplicated in Nagasaki. Over two hundred and ten thousand people, who woke up those mornings not expecting to die, were killed in an eye-blink of time. A month later, a typhoon impacted Hiroshima flooding the balance of their remains. The surviving population was stunned, decimated of all thought and hope. Their emotions filled with an extreme emptiness and sadness, beyond all human comprehension.

While sifting through the carnage at both sites, a handful of visionaries created a concept churning out 30 master rebuilding plans for repair. Some of these numbers wanted to move the surviving populations into the nearby mountains; to leave the radioactive rubble alone to serve as a monument to man's inhumanity to man. Winston Churchill said at the time that "the idiot child now has new matches to play with." Such was the destructive vent and emotionally charged mentality of the time. The United States eventually saw things differently.

Human nature influenced by God's grace (to offset our self-abuse natures) then created a more compassionate overview for repair. Man's ingenuity and creativeness surfaced, with mankind learning from its own ignorance. The by-product of using a technology whose end product produced overwhelming guilt.

After several months of planning the United States initiated the Marshall Plan tying in W. Edwards Deming's 14 points of quality control. This evolved the devastated cities five decades later into what they are today. Both cities are now thriving metropolises, built on the human spirit of hope and ingenuity, with man working with man incorporating business enterprise. The Japanese took from this incident, a horrendous tragedy and transferred bad to good, developing their own concept for repair. By utilizing the best of all worlds, learning from the events that led to this destruction, and with our financial assistance they were able to formally marry their corporate world, education and political enterprises together, learning from their past mistakes. They banded together transforming a human made disaster into success

When our European ancestors landed in this country they were leaving a past filled with secular patterns of leadership duplicating history, eventually forcing them into dramatic change. They were humbled and ill prepared for the onslaught of the unknown and its adversity. Because of this, and the overwhelming odds of possible failure, they were aided by God's guidance, grace and His parental love. This Almighty Power is a benevolent parent fulfilling a "He and She" role in our upbringing and this nation's history.

He created Socrates, who educated Plato, who then mentored Aristotle, laying the foundations for new concepts and ideas. Their concerns and intuitions created opportunity, overcoming adversity through self-education and listening to their inner voices. This instilled creative thought in other's conscious minds. This growth and spiritual enlightenment eventually led to the foundations and thinking of our Western World.

History has shown that each new concept and idea evolves from the inspiration of one person eventually having an effect on others, be it in the boardroom of corporate America to convince us to spend our money; or Christ or Mohammed or Buddha affecting the thinking of the religious world, or a Mahatma Gandhi, Mikhail Gorbachov and Franklin Roosevelt affecting political and social reform in their respective countries.

Since God continually speaks to each one of us, they, through their common sense and a spiritual probing were willing to listen to what was being said to their conscious minds and do something with this message. With intuitive reasoning and becoming motivated by what they felt internally, they placed their beliefs and imaginations into the lives and the thought processes of their immediate populations. Their mutual failures were to not think further ahead to reach the hearts and souls of those who would be instrumental in its continuation.

In this modern era we, like those who went before us, are duplicating this same path of moving into the unknown, like Columbus and these men, not fully cognizant of where we are going. We are being asked through these same intuitions, based on faith and common sense, to listen to our times, let go, and allow God's will to be done through our actions. To not fear for the future, but learn from our past, in confronting the challenges and difficulties of our times with a reasonable level of confidence and a major level of trust.

When we do not think things through, we mimic the factors of what created a problem. We go off half-baked, taking what could be salvaged and destroy any positive resolution. We lose sight of the energies and history that went into each event, causing our current historical repetitions. We are now confronted with breaking this cycle, or what will be started, will historically be destroyed from within, duplicating itself once again.

Realizing that a formal proposal for a conscious human change is an alien thought for most of us, the balance of these words being used is to initiate new conceptual thought and future conversation. To think out these few points covered, using our past history as reference and do a little more thinking each day; as human life should be an interplay taking the best of what each moment offers. Each of us should realize that we have been continually blessed, and out of this, we should live our lives with simplicity and spiritual focus on the Power that created all.

The future is, and always will be, dependent on each of us making a compassionate commitment to take a personal responsibility for each of our actions. We will need to embrace the concept that each thought and deed we commit to in assisting another, affects them for their lifetime. For if we help one then that turns into two. One generation to the next generation forever. Out of this, we learn to look at each other as a child of God and as our relations, brothers and sisters we did not personally choose. In doing this, we can develop a compassionate empathy and care for our neighbor and planet using Him for our continual guidance.

The initial step for correction will require the recognition that our nation today is based on a reactive "me" instead of "we" mentality; conditioned to keep what it has, usually wanting more, siphoning off the assets provided for our children's lifetimes. Each of us will need a reasonable path which will broaden our understanding, that will lead into an eventual acceptance that our manmade disasters are now life threatening. And then, when informed, to become internally motivated to be part of the overall answer.

With this in mind, it will be necessary to know where one has been, know where one is now, and to know where one is eventually going to avoid going around in the circles of life with history consistently, repeating itself. We will need some type of roadmap to eventually choose what we want and where we want to go, and know how much fuel we have in the tank. Then outline an itinerary to aid us in staying on the correct route, as most of us would not go on a trip or long journey without planning the final destination.

As with all things in life, we sometimes choose the fast pace of the interstate highway system, or most scenic roads, rail and trails. We would like to know the budget determining the over all costs to see what is affordable in time, effort and money. We would also determine where would stay and for how long, and in what accommodations.

To establish a plan for programmed change will require a preplanning similar to this journey for our future lives. A travel where we, the general public, will decide democratically where we want to go, continuing the processes of our human evolution dealing with our bumps and turns. And to then believe that our Creator would have nothing less, as we have been provided with all of the internal and spiritual mechanisms to have this happen out of His unconditional love.

From our past experiences we can realize that our current world is riddled with compromise, ego and personal agendas eventually convoluting the original intentions of our Father. It can be recognized that we have not been educated to think in the long-term, the decisions we make as a human society. Many excellent ideas of some very bright people never come into fruition because any concept for change translates into personal and political discomfort. We resist change, fearful of its effects and the unknown trying to control the outcome creating our setbacks and political interferences. We can also learn from others and what they accomplished with belief and vision, creating a tremendous new vocational enterprise.

We know from our personal experiences that bad habits are hard to break unless we are totally committed to change what has been ingrained over time. We have a duplicative history of a "two steps forward, three steps backward" approach similar to a drug addict or alcoholic. It is our current human nature to fall back on our past experiences rather than to accept alterations to our comfort levels. The engine to address this effort for these reasons will still be money and more importantly, our Father's will, to reach the personal level of acceptance.

This overall plan will have to simultaneously address our many divisions, taking politics out of our lives while minimizing our emotional objections and human fears. This journey's itinerary could outline the "cause and effect" issues, then encapsulate what has been broken, or is breaking; the ecology and our educational systems then tying in our family dysfunctions, to include the damaging effects of our governmental intrusions.

By outlining their histories and current status, these factors can be placed into four separate but equal programs to be addressed with suggested, then implemented, remedies for public discussion. All of the problems we have are integrated within these four specific areas. All have the real possibility of healing themselves through democratic action, utilizing our intelligence and free will.

Because we have a human need to clearly see what we are getting into, this is but a small suggestion of allowing God to move through each one of us, addressing what we have created. An initial proposal to develop a comfort level to pool the talent and energies of America's corporate board of directors, which is we, to eventually embrace the concept and need for repair.

Any societal transition of the magnitude being discussed in this writing will require each of us as God's children to listen through our inner imaginations, respecting the sovereignty and overall purpose of human life. Mortal persons who will be unselfishly inspired and able to leave their egos and fears out of the equation and are open to listening to their thoughts and hearts through God. Basically taking a leap of faith, trusting in His existence and their personal direction, allowing His will to be done.

This book is just one person's perception of a world that is now in danger of imploding and is based on one's intuitive concerns, based on the emotions personally felt on September 11. It is also one of many versions that each of us will be continually receiving, in an attempt to wake up our various generations to start listening and doing things differently. This is just a small part of a larger set of dynamics to strike a resonate cord, to have each of us listen to our inner self, then do something with the message. And it bears repeating, and can not be stressed enough, that if what is being heard brings harm to any living creature including oneself, then what is being heard is wrong.

In creating and planning for future alterations we have much to learn from history. We should recognize that it has taken 50 years to gradually assemble this current existence with our social and moral problems, our current indebtedness and a democracy out of control. We will need to also realize that there will be no short-term solutions, no quick fix, or magic wand to address our personal needs -- and the universal demands of the Earth.

We can embrace the same concept described above, but on a much broader global scale. We can emulate the same belief systems of the Japanese and the Americans who implemented this reformation fifty years ago.

We have the same, if not superior, ability of those master planners to fix what we know to be failing. We can take from what is currently being experienced, the breakdowns of the Earth's ecological systems, the growing dysfunctions of our business community and family unit, and the desperate need of an educational overhaul, by blending in much of we have immorally done to ourselves into new avenues of thought.

We can fall back on our professional conditioning of the 1960s and 1970s, when we were encouraged to semi-plan our tomorrows. At that time it was not unusual to be asked by our schoolteachers and professional mentors to create a step-by-step process in planning objectives to develop some final goal. We were taught by innovated business methods to think in logical progressions of thought. What we were not taught at the time was to understand the dynamics of the dollar on politics and the dilution and corruption of our national ideals in what we were creating.

To address these integrated issues, we will need to think in little-step terms, moving into the crawling stages of our acceptance process. Then with ethical checks and balances in place, and once we are comfortable with this transition, to start the first step from within; then growing more dependent on the grace and love of our Father. All future planning will take a small group of talented, compassionate persons to weather the storms of our ingrained objections and fear of the unknown.

Turning this world around will have to be established through our hearts and minds, eventually implemented by our business and educational communities with visionary focus for evaluation and performance to plan. Planning and future standards of human compassion and morality will require the involvement of our religious institutions and non-profit organizations. Each person, involved in this, will need to understand the much larger picture, and the responsibilities we have to our Creator.

In this we will need to come to realization that to break historical repetition, this program in its entirety will have to be initiated at the "grass-roots" level for long-term impact. The distractive influences of contrived political interference and public misinformation will have to be anticipated, then minimized as many governing officials have been conditioned into a turf-protection mentality. Over 700 billion dollars of our nation's present annual expenditures could be transferred to the expertise of the non-profit private sector, if so elected to underwrite the initial cost. Over 41 cents of every tax dollar is lost and wasted on inefficiency and the pork-barreling corruptions of our government services.

CHAPTER XIII
THE PLAN

History has shown that positive progressions for man's evolution are frequently short-circuited because of the lack of long-term focus backed with consistent faith, then becoming corrupted from within. The concepts for repair and reorganization have taken place, but on a smaller scale of implementation.

The League of Nations, The Marshall Plan, the United Nations, N.A.T.O. and all of our social programs would be close, but it will take the combination of all plus a religious rebirth to move us positively into the 22nd century. It will require all so moved, to place this in small steps for conceptualizing with an open mind, leading into an eventual touching within our souls, then to our minds. It will also require a consistent internal listening within our hearts as the doorway to our souls, slowly relating to what is being said, staying out of God's way in allowing this to happen.

We should realize that never in the history of our recorded time has any nation or civilization accomplished so much damage in this short period of time, or taken on a project of this dimension and depth to the best of our current knowledge. This is one plausible step for correction, with the understanding that we will all be, and should be, initially skeptical of the eventual outcome.

Thousands of books, documentaries and movies have shown or taught us not only the beauty of God's creation but the many horrors we have caused in our secular world. We are moved by much of what we see and feel at that moment, but lose contact as these visual effects are soon replaced with other visual images. Because we are bombarded with so much negative information so quickly, the input becomes blurred, rapidly replaced by another atrocity of humankind's reaction to the world in which we live: a secularized world filled with over 160 regional wars globally, with parents now killing their children and vice versa, with mass human genocide lightly taken.

The growing inefficiencies of our now all-intrusive government, the dysfunctions of the family unit and the inability of the educational community to teach us how to think in logical thought, combined are the root cause of our social divisions. Each step towards a remedy will require a simultaneous programmed approach incorporating all three social areas, as they are intertwined and interrelated, with our present evolution far removed from what God originally intended.

Today it is difficult to stay focused on any one thing, let alone think about the problems of the entire Earth. Because of this, we are finding ourselves in a conscious need to think at a much slower, intuitive pace. Each of us will have to open ourselves to think with a logical progression of thought.

In this process we will need to examine the history and cause of each problem and its current set of energies and dynamics. We will have to minimize our emotional reactions and current nearsightedness, which historically clouds the opportunities for positive and long-lasting planned change.

By visualizing what the Earth's conditions could be 50 years from now (both good and bad) would open the doors to new thinking, thus altering our future perceptions. Each step is going to take a transformation of revising our doubts to an opened mind filled with our human imaginations, and our willingness to allow God's will to surface. Then to eventually use one's present stature and our human relationships to affect a long-term outcome. Our motivations would be our personal survival, our children's futures and to break the repetitious patterns that destroy us from within.

This process would open the many unused doors that are available through our Father. We would be able to democratically use our free spirits and wills in being of service to not only ourselves, but to all of humankind. By allowing ourselves to become His vassals we could identify, then visualize what we have done to ourselves, and this planet over these past 50 years.

A business analyst, in examining the problems within a company, delves into the total history and operations of the business structure, as previously mentioned. It is a thorough physical of the totals of input, throughput and output of each operating area that make the company a whole. The process examines the strength and weakness in its total makeup, which results in the final product and a profit to the owner and/or stockholder.

The first step in this examination is to interview the founder of the company and upper management to gain an initial overview, determining the overall goals and final objectives. From this the operating chemistry is determined, along with the philosophies of structure and ownership's wants and needs. I have found that, with over 600 individual analyses personally conducted over a 25-year period over 90% of all company problems are created because of management's miscommunication to the employees.

The second step is to do a spreadsheet financial analysis of the company's past 5 years of operations, examining how the money is earned, invested and spent. Concurrently, a questionnaire is handed to all the employees, in total confidence, to get their take on the strengths and weaknesses of each area of operation. They will oftentimes see the same things as management, but from a different perspective.

The third step is to then digest the input from these three levels, tying this into a physical walk-through of the company's entire operational structure. A findings meeting is established, discussing the conclusions with the client, not disclosing the human resources input. From this, profit leaks and the "cause and effect" of the operational inefficiencies are identified with proposed solutions and a time frame suggested. This establishes a reorganization and re-engineering outline, an overall business plan with a monitored operating budget.

A business plan places the overall objective on paper to initiate thought and discussion. This establishes a written visual overview outlining the overall objectives and the steps needed to have it happen. The plan produces the history of cause and effect with the need for expansion, alteration or dramatic change for market penetration. It anticipates the strengths and weakness of the objective, similar to how a home would be initially blueprinted by an architect for eventual use by the building contractor, and in turn used by the contractor planning the steps with the subcontractors and then the laborer putting the pieces together.

As we think out plans for making this World better, it might be helpful to think of all of us as homebuilders planning for structural change. As a contractor would construct a new house advanced planning is initiated to minimize a waste of time and money eventually placing the pieces together. These following words and chapters will take this same premise in transitioning your present doubts and reservations, into a new realm for understanding. A plan about where we can go as a human society using God as our architect; and we the laborers repairing our mutual home, better known as planet Earth.

The overall objective and mission statement would be an initial concept of the populations of the world eventually working together in unison, living in peace and prosperity as the overall goal; identifying, then listing what we have done and allowed to be developed, and how we plan to correct it. This model would initially be created in theory, using secular terminology and tying in human ingenuity.

A formal picture would be developed using one's imagination, outlining the overall objectives and initial goals with the pluses and negatives visually pictured then physically projected. A step-by-step outline of the procedures and time frame would be developed, analyzing the cause and effect of each level undertaken. In the process, a creation of a blueprint or business plan spelling out the, who, what, where, when and whys with an initial picture developed. This would incorporate the costs of manpower and materials with a forecasted time of completion.

In developing a comprehensive overview of what is to be developed, a vista and schedule are projected and used for bid requests from the area's builders as an example. A prospective buyer will research the background and experience of the person who will be in charge and weigh the different estimates and the talents of the candidates. Once the decision is made for the final construction there is an initial meeting with the client, architect and the general contractor who walks the project through step-by-step. The process develops a clear understanding of who is going to be responsible for completing the project, anticipating any potential problems before they happen.

In the case of a home being built, the initial frame of the structure is pictured, with visual overlays reproducing the individual steps to provide a finished overview through computer-aided design. Through this communication, a human chemistry is developed with each person getting to know the other, establishing a comfort and trust level. The legal regulations are met, permits are acquired, the financing completed through a lending institution and the foundation is initially installed. Prior to the concrete being poured there is an anticipation of future need and alterations. The electricians and plumbers and foundation workers are coordinated before any other work is accomplished. Do less and all efforts to this point end up being wasted, creating a need for duplication of effort, destroying what has been accomplished.

From the foundation, outside supporting walls are built with roof trusses delivered on time. The exterior shell is then coated with protective materials. The roof is papered and shingled and the outside walls sealed. The movement is then coordinated for indoor construction with the bathrooms and kitchen taking the normal priority. All sinks, toilets, bathtubs, electrical outlets and their supporting hardware have been ordered in advance and scheduled for just in time delivery. The balance of the home, the living and bedroom and other amenities are then finished in a logical progression of order.

If the buyer keeps his or her change orders to a minimum, the house will be brought in on time and hopefully on budget, weather permitting. There are allowances for changes in the project through its completion. It is realized that human nature is quite changeable in not knowing what the client thinks he wants. Even the best of plans normally go awry.

When a CEO of a company initiates a long and short-range business plan, these steps are duplicated, but the terminology becomes a bit more sophisticated. All steps and responsibilities for reaching objectives are clearly understood by all pertinent personnel and measured by performance to plan. An organizational flowchart is clearly structured with all individuals working together in tandem.

Key management is provided the road map to perform a functional step-by-step analysis to assign accountability to all personnel during the implementation of a project. A step-by-step process surgically details the procedures before they become a problem. Constant flexibility is required as we live in a stochastic world filled with constant change.

Each area of responsibility is identified establishing standards of performance with delegation and procedures clearly defined. Management is then personally involved in the process, developing the product with responsibilities clearly understood. This allows the concept to be born and to mature, resulting in the finished idea.

Key personnel are given a planned budget to work with utilizing cash-flow management. This allows each person in charge to anticipate the costs for the work done. As the driving incentive, they are rewarded for bringing the project in under cost. The customer then receives what has been supplied, hopefully satisfied with the end product, and pays the bill. The company then, if properly planned, generates a profit to pay off on the risk and to invest in other areas.

Most successful companies stress teamwork and communications. The employees are involved in the day-to-day decisions, and form an integrated style of management. A round table is used for discussion to minimize lost focus and misdirection. The optimally run company is one that will run with leadership taking a constant vacation. Many fail because leadership doesn't want or know how to let go, or they do not communicate the final picture or objective well, causing confusion and failure. For all the above reasons the following is provided to open a personal discussion within ourselves, and hopefully our Father.

THE OBJECTIVE - *Visualize yourself flying over the United States at 200 miles high in space. The year is 2050. Looking down, you see various forms of quilted green space; the balance of the land interspersed with pristine, fresh water lakes, rivulets, rivers and salt-water oceans. Upon closer inspection, you see numerous communities with a population base numbering 50,000-100,000 family homes and symmetrically designed support services. The paved strips of the nation's highway systems now support a monorail system interlocked nationwide with high-speed rail for transportation services.*

The medians of once worn-out interstate systems now house underground, fiberoptic utility lines, and aqueducts for energy transference and water. The older cities are a visual mosaic outlined with oaks, pine, spruce and elm. The land is systematically planned out, representing a patchwork quilt with harmonious consistency. You sense that utmost consideration is given to protecting the natural habitat, the trees, wetlands and the marsh systems, which supply each community's fresh water, developing numerous cottage industries. Farming methods and residential abuses were altered with the use of pesticides, herbicides and other manmade poisons including polluting fertilizers minimized and eventually discontinued.

You recall that several years earlier the once burned-out, eroded land was replenished with nutrient rich silt from the polluted lakes, rivers and streams and the balance of the nation's waterways — naturally digesting the waste of the industrial age. The silt blended into the soil producing lush agricultural areas interspersed with parks and recreational facilities. The waterways you now view, are now clean enough to swim in, providing mankind with all the challenges and outdoor activity that any human would desire with each community becoming the sportsman's Mecca known throughout the world.

Because of a spiritual reawakening, established not too long ago, all religious practitioners use the philosophies of the Peace and Glastonbury Abbeys as the initial foundation, utilizing mentors of all faiths to bridge the old gaps of interpretative differences creating their turf wars. All human pain and despondency became a single focus with the understanding that each society is only as strong as its weakest member. That cause and effect of human misery is now easily identified and addressed with common sense solution making for the love for all of mankind. All religious organizations have come to the understanding that all human life is a gift from our single Maker and humankind shares a unifying energy of worshiping the same God, through prayer and meditation, with little need for outside human intervention.

The change was formally instituted in the early 2000s, which provided the energies and talent as an institution for enlightenment and spiritual growth. Throughout the nation's communities and eventually nationwide, personnel from the private sector are now working hand in hand with our local high schools, colleges, universities and vocational institutions to educate, train and retrain people, addressing four basic areas of re-engineering our current infrastructure.

Planning and zoning departments on the local level and electronically linked nationwide are now continually working with the business communities, social organizations, educational, environmental and social architects who make far-reaching decisions of what would and could be developed, with each entity addressing the past makeup of the cause and effect of a nation simply losing its focus on God. Fire, law enforcement, education, the D.O.T. and the utility companies forecasts are incorporated into each decision affecting the outcome using prayer and God's guidance for direction. Eventually the monies spent on incarcerating human beings were invested in long-term educational reform.

All public departments, religious organizations and the non-profit sector constantly provide the vision and sweat equity in addressing each community's social needs. An electronically linked complex acting as a collecting magnet and information clearing house, poised for the utilization of man's thoughts and idea making, and natural creativeness, a new vision of a peaceful war machine.

The inner spirit and human energies of the cities and urban life are renewed in the transformation with self-esteem replacing human despondency. It is a concept, well-planned and provided for, learning from the mistakes of our predecessors. Human values naturally improved from this intelligent process of planning and implementation, creating the existence that our Creator originally intended.

METHODOLOGY - Each community throughout this country and world has persons who are bucking the tides of social conformity and trends. Human beings, such as you or I, who do not like what they see and recognize the need for change. They may be the head of a church, temple or synagogue counseling the psychological and spiritual need of each parishioner or drug addict, or assisting the need of a lost soul, or they may be a member of a non-profit organization addressing the integrity of the ecology, fighting off the developers and landowners need for short-term profit taking at the expense of one's quality of life. There are others who serve the needs of education as a school board member, teacher or a volunteer assistant or join parent/teacher or health organizations, dissatisfied with the product being produced. Or they may be interested in developing political solutions and run for office outside of main stream politics, seeking to right an injustice, understanding many of the human issues.

It may be a small business owner or corporate executive who provides employment for others while improving their personal income and life, or it may be a single mother or housewife or maintenance worker holding down two jobs to keep their families together in spite of all opposing odds. Or it may be a political diplomat negotiating peace between two warring factions, or it may be you or a firefighter, policeman or medic coming to the aid of others. Together they and all the rest of us are the plausible answer to addressing our many horrendous problems, allowing God back into our lives. The Bible states that 144,000 kindred spirits have the potential of affecting the thinking and changing the actions of the entire world.

Through marketing, education and visualization each of us can be motivated by an inner commitment and concern about our current quality of life, and the world we will be leaving to our grandchildren. Organizational and focus meetings can bring our current and local ideas together with the country's successful organizations and personnel under a single umbrella approach rectifying much of what we have done. The findings could then be incorporated on a state, then regional and national basis for a gradual global implementation. The visualization outlined in this chapter could be the initial model, eventually creating an overview of our entire nation's, and the world's, various human care programs, their issues, histories and their current status.

Organizational platforms and their issues would be identified which are productive and cost-effective in developing social and spiritual change. In essence, a well thought out architectural code and bipartisan vision structured to initially permeate the nation and eventually the rest of the world over the next 50 years. The initial objective is to create an all-encompassing overview of our current problems divided into four categorical areas of importance, understanding their underlying needs. All are equal to the other, and are interrelated to the majority of the difficulties we share.

- One would be the ecology and resource planning; as if we lose the integrity of the inner workings of our communities and the Earth all else is not important.
- Two would be education, for without becoming educated we would not be able to recognize that we have any major problems.
- Three would be the re-establishment of family values and the family unit, to eventually create compassionate and concerned adults and productive offspring.
- And four would be the downsizing of governments on all levels, re-establishing our founders' original intent of allowing each of our country's citizens to become responsible for his and her personal destinies.

The concept would eventually be publicly and privately funded (through matching governing grants, personal tithing, corporate donations and income derived from the services rendered), utilizing the media for public education, anticipating what the future holds in store. Each step would identify the "cause and effect" presented in an educating and entertaining format outlining the many issues with a prudent number of suggested cures.

There are many excellent ideas and concepts provided by all generations never allowed to come into fruition. The "status quo" mentality is constantly surfacing in our current world. For this reason all common sense applications would encompass this reality. The business and political communities through this transition can be enlightened to embrace this re-engineering, improving the quality of life, with the educational sector honing the availability of a highly skilled labor force. In essence, the public and private sectors working together to improve upon the pristine beauty of the country, producing an abundance of natural life, with new employment opportunities altering the way we currently do things.

With prayerful thought, and the use of looking in the long-term, our intuitions can be utilized in developing a strong, corporate asset-use program, and a 50-year ongoing plan that can eventually be accepted by local and state leadership supported by a grass-roots approach. Planning and zoning departments on the city and county level could evolve to work with the business and educational community, making far reaching projections that limited what land would be developed; land-banking the county's fragile areas, protecting the ecology and the percolating systems that recharged each communities resources for fresh water. All civic and social organizations can be housed in a centralized area utilizing the networking capabilities of the Internet in addressing human social problems, etc.

The timing and format could resemble the following. It is imperative that all participants know the history of our current situations, where they are now and where they are heading, then project the overall human costs.

Step I — Each committee (in these four areas for reformation) would initiate the process through public presentations, then forming a consensus combining the ideas, current programs, concepts, wants and needs in a community town meeting format. By examining the cause and effect of each existing program and the infrastructure in place and by prioritizing the input, a long-range business plan and a time frame for initiation would then create the first step of conscious thought.

A lead committee would outline all of the information obtained, listing all known issues, and would conduct an in-depth review with each information source addressing each person's individual concerns with all activities publicized. All differing views would be included with the differences mediated with egos and personality conflicts left outside the door. Validity and cost effectiveness would need to be thoroughly examined.

Step II — A spreadsheet analysis and 20-year financial projection would need to be incorporated using the past 20 years of our country's and private sector's tracking of profit and loss by area of responsibility. This would create a forecasted operating budget to assess future savings and expense. Past variable and fixed expense profit leaks would be identified with remedies suggested, the initial savings generated by eliminating the duplication of effort.

Constant flexibility would be required as past and current programs and commitments, including Social Security, Medicare, Medicaid and all health care programs of the White House and Congress would be phased down over a 20-50 year period. The history of turf protection will need to be addressed. Future impact will have to be anticipated, moving all human programs of agriculture, health, education, defense and human welfare to the expertise of the private and military sectors.

Step III — Schedule public participation incorporating the ideas generated from the initial forums to address each community's, and the country's, pressing difficulties in restoring the ecology, educational reform, family and parental counseling and the downsizing of government responsibility. Obtain state and local governments involvement, then federal as all elected officials including our President and Cabinet, Congress, the Supreme Court, governors, mayors and county commissioners and city councils will be part of the overall solution.

Incorporate all findings, and then prioritize by field area, staying focused on the overall goal throughout all proceedings. Involve the media to constantly educate and include the general public.

As one of two examples, growth management can be tied in to possible concurrence with each community's infrastructure in place before any additional residential and commercial development is allowed. Creative thinking can evolve into an embraced philosophy that property owners, developers and general contractors also have social and moral responsibilities to their following generations, and in doing the right things for their immediate community that their income and property values will increase with compliance.

Another is to recognize that our family dysfunctions start with the child, duplicating what they experienced during their upbringing. Parenting and relationship skills are currently an on the job experience creating tremendous violence and control issues. Today men and women are insensitive to the common respect we should have for each other as human beings. When addressed early in a child's life, this conditioning can be countered with a common awareness, which over two to three generations can mature into a civility to each other as adults.

Step IV — All existing for profit and non-profit executives including the Board of Directors should be interviewed to get their take on each social and government program assessing their strength and weaknesses. This due diligence and audit process will examine future growth opportunities and examine human attitudes in determining future personnel development and training needs for development.

Step V — An optional essay questionnaire should be given to all employees of each organization and governmental department with total confidentiality assured. This is to identify the future acceptance of change, and will identify any internal weakness that may have been overlooked by management in altering existing programs.

Step VI — Public participation. Review past and current results of studies conducted over the past 50 years as many solutions have been accomplished but not implemented.

Step VII — Formulate findings of all the above into simplified written presentation for public discussion with a thorough examination of the programs intent, how it was well or poorly managed, and how the weakness will be corrected.

Step VIII — Develop continual media and newspaper coverage encouraging public participation with a prudent sense of urgency.

Step IX — Open debate. Then initiate on a county, then state, then regional basis. Implement and test the various programs by region, then by taking the best implement on a national basis utilizing the Internet for information exchange.

CHAPTER XIV
CREATIVITY

From the inception of fire, steel and the wheel, mankind has continually been an innovative lot, the Phoenix rising from the ashes of failure. Forty years ago we were able to place men on the moon based on a president's inspiration coupled with the imaginations of talented scientists and the construction feats of a handful of engineers. Because of their imaginations and willingness to think on a larger scale, we are now able to view our celestial neighbors through the Hubble Telescope. We are finally realizing that we are surrounded by systematic chaos, yet sense of order, unfathomable to the human mind.

This process, being a double-edged sword, has allowed us to realize what we can accomplish using our talents and abilities to overcome the unknown. It has also shown us how frail and precarious and special life is on this planet Earth, and how much we really do not know.

The first part of this book outlined some of what we have accomplished and demolished over the past 50 years because of these factors. The morning of September 11 is a representative message of our secular divisions from our Father bringing out our strengths, compassion and weaknesses, and the dark side of man.

Our current wars, domestic terrorism, political ineptitude, mass human despair, and ecological waste represent our ignorance of mankind not thinking on a higher ground, not listening well to ourselves. We are now living in a growing disillusioned and malfunctioning world with so much happening around us that we are having difficultly in believing that we can internally correct our many challenges with common sense intelligence and compassion. A description of a world that is far from what our Father intended, with us losing sight of our original purpose, not feeling or thinking with our inner souls.

If one could imagine the past expenditure of ten trillion dollars spent on our military-industrial complex over these past four decades, being redirected over the next 40 years for a peaceful evolution, one would think that we would have a good chance to financially buy the corrective path. But with our personal, financial and emotional challenges and history of our political and corporate manipulation, it would be difficult to see a positive light at the end of this journey, as this, too, would become corrupted and abused with history repeating itself.

The balance of this thought process is just part of a plausible answer to add to our maturing processes; to hopefully have us start thinking things out, breaking our patterns of negative historical repetitions. It is not designed to create additional divisions and hardships but to have us recognize our "cause and effect" on a personal level.

As said earlier, God uses each one of us in an unexplainable manner and time. I, along with everyone involved in the creation of what you are reading, are just a few of His vehicles now being used for His purpose. I sense that He is most concerned about what we are doing to ourselves, which is the underlying purpose of this manuscript, because this writing is far away from what I would normally do. I believe that He realizes our various strengths, and in His own manner trusts that eventually we will do the right things while we are here.

I am sure that He also realizes that, because of our human conditioning, all changes and thoughts for change will always have to come from within each one of us to have a lasting effect. For this reason I believe that He wants each one of us to do our thinking for ourselves, with a universal God working through us as the altruistic answer. His existence provides each of us with His grace, miracle working, love, compassion and continual guidance. In the long-term, trying to protect most of us from doing more damage to ourselves, and with this knowledge to eventually grow through this era of growing disasters, spiritually and emotionally.

Our religious structures, nationally and worldwide, will need to place themselves and the entire world into continual prayer, opening their own souls for direction. All should embrace the reality that the words they use and their methodologies keep us separated and divided with their interpretative doctrines.

With God's guidance and a renewed focus with less arrogance, the multitudes of organizations worldwide can bring us together as the children we are. There is not one religion that is pure or precise in cornering the market on God, and it would be arrogant to think so. The only true path, to understand and live with our Father's presence, will come from each one of listening and feeling within our souls. To open our hearts and minds to His continual message, then embrace the original purpose for our existence; eventually becoming the primary vehicles and catalysts bringing man together in a peace. Then to overcome our past human differences by altering what we currently perceive to be the truth.

There are and will be new and expressive methods of developing new chapters and options in this evolution, but each step will have to be initiated from within, with each of us seeking spiritual direction for our own spiritual development. Even God's son, while He was on this Earth, was not able to have His voice and vision heard with a total acceptance, which is something that we and all of our secular based religions will eventually have to learn to overcome. A blending of our human divisions can be approached with the knowledge that all persons from all nations worship and have the same one Creator — perhaps mirroring the philosophies of the Peace and Glastonbury Abbeys, establishing human order on this earth.

An ether and Entity who loves each one of us with all of His being and trusts that we will evolve into a higher evolution of understanding will be the master point in this equation. That what God originally created may be addressed with a composite of compassion, love and the understanding of our differences while consciously recognizing our sameness and that He personally speaks to each one of us constantly.

Today there are over 3,000 names applied to the existence of our same Father which will need to be brought together with a sense of unconditional love and private prayer in overcoming our self-induced conflicts and weaknesses as man. Jesus Christ and our Western religions are not a single method of this transformation and enlightenment, but could prove to be the common catalyst to move forward. The prophets, rabbis, sages, angels and the masters of all God based foundations are part of the larger message, confirming God's existence of creation and His personal love.

All the moral codes and positive motivations of the world come through the efforts of believers driven by their faith and their spiritual evolution in this thought process. Most decisions driven by an inner sense, initiated by one's consciousness, can create hope for a better tomorrow providing for a positive progression for man. Whatever the outcomes of our future, our decisions will have to be accomplished through our democratic process and our personal faith, allowing dramatic change when personally elected then incorporate our natural born gifts and talents, working towards a common goal of remembering the purpose of our Genesis.

The following thoughts are not to micro- or macro-manage the input or the result, but are provided to allow for a possible spiritual reawakening and restructuring of discussion and future thought for change. We are now in our early stages of becoming aware that there is a universal positive energy in which good can prevail over bad, once we learn how to tap into this positive resource.

Because of our history of sharing, innovation, diversity, agility and wealth, we are the only nation at the present time that has the capability of influencing the rest of the world in this evolution. Few others have the will or the wherewithal to induce this transition in an all-encompassing, benevolent manner. Through our imaginations and intuition we can transform our current .22 caliber mentality into a .357 magnum mind, a positive program reinventing ourselves. Today we have the opportunity to right some of our many wrongs, using this age of technology and our doing things differently, recognizing 911 as our wake-up call. To eventually advance in a national memorial to the many human lives lost or destroyed over our nation's many years.

The following scenario is not to be interpreted as an all-encompassing panacea, but as an initial semi-detailed architectural plan to build from. It is structured to have us think out the future for our children's children, and to recognize our large parenting responsibilities.

All of us are now confronted with overcoming our "turf protection" and our ignoring the world's true conditions; and to rearrange our consumptive natures, establishing higher priorities. To write, direct and produce a blueprint for our own individual and mutual survival — corporately. To use our ingenuity and creative abilities, envisioning many, if not all of our human potential.

****

We are learning that our human minds and our social behavior are influenced and eventually conditioned by what we see, hear and play. Human behavior, our movements, thoughts and emotions are transformed into our thinking minds, eventually evolving into our consumptive and reactive habits. We laugh and cry and are transitionally moved by what we experience on the screen or by the music digested eventually absorbing this stimulus.

What we experience from being the audience leaves lasting impressions, affecting our personal conditioning, the creating our social habits. The strings are pulled on our inner psyche moving us into our reactions enhanced by a subconscious conceptualization. The animated and printed message — human, machine originated and cartoon generated — has the tremendous potential of massively affecting our eventual behavior through comedy, song and drama to guide the paths of correction and change.

The entertainment industry can be utilized in conjunction with an overall plan to reverse the current paths it presently mirrors, to eventually alter our current thinking and our nation's future development. The minds, hearts and souls of this world of distraction and information could be stretched in developing pre-designed programs to eventually reach a viewer's mind. Instead of selling a product for quick profit taking and human consumption, thought can be given to the psychological impact of what is being generated.

We are in the early stages of understanding that the mind and our psyches are easily influenced by what we see, sense and feel. This eventually creates our good and bad reactions to how we perceive things, later becoming ingrained into our human society. Past movies although focused on popular themes of dinosaurs and comic book characters, as examples, also informs us of DNA and the dangerous manipulations conducted by our life sciences. When we read of human and animal cloning this past information surfaces through our awakened awareness.

Action movies and love stories, their messages enhanced by music, have the conscious ability to mark the positives instead of the negatives in our human reactions. By transitioning evil and violence off the screen with compassion and tolerance over a period of a decade or less would have the real potential of creating a more understanding and less violent world.

Via the Internet, games, music and short-stories with a mass audience appeal could be combined into our societal reprogramming with a focused marketing and advertising plan, then work in tandem with magazines, newspaper and television documentaries, re-enforcing the scope of the message.

The family unit on all socioeconomic levels could be envisioned with the times and trials of attempting to survive our day, dealing with the demands of trying to provide for themselves and the care of their aging parents while supporting the needs of their children. There could be a ringleader in his or her late 80s, leading a number of retirees living in a retirement center, holding wheelchair races and trying to escape their worlds of involuntary imprisonment. Perhaps by portraying an understanding that with birth and death, we don't pay attention to who lies next to us, and that our racial differences and bigotry with others start in early childhood via peer and parental pressure, could initiate an attitude and acceptance reprogramming.

Thought could be given to our being a convoluted melting pot. A nation controlled and influenced by our circumstances could be imaged, bringing us into a mutual understanding that each person has a good and also bad story to tell. Organized religions on all fronts along with education and media programming could be coordinated with additional human themes bringing the messages to our hearts. Religious structures, newspapers, talk radio and music, magazines, television and the movie screen working in a moral unison, portraying the "cause and effect" of a specific situation with suggested alternations.

Future writers could phase out profanity, violence, sex, rape and drugs, murder, suicide and satanic themes from their current methods of development. Underground lines of fiber-optics, lasers and computer hardware and software can be married in this composition. Spielberg's, Sorkin's, Lucas's and Howard's enormous talent of manipulating images on the screen could eventually produce a kinder more informed society, added to the Oprahs, Joseph Campbells and Dr. Wayne Dyers of this world.

By emphasizing that we are all someone's child, a series of larger messages, advertisements, articles, short and long television programming and movies could instill the belief that the public at large will profit from a strong thriving family living together in love. Each generation has much to learn from the other, creating a sense of purpose for our children's futures and that death is not to be feared, but is part of our ongoing spiritual evolution.

In tandem, on the political and social front, all welfare and parenting programs can be combined into an educational curriculum to provide a concise, direct overview of what programs are working locally and worldwide with a strong mentoring message.

With the media presenting the human effect in an entertaining way, elder and childcare can be combined. A grandparent can mentor the energies and love of a child with both profiting from this interaction. The child can learn respect, discipline and love from the alternative parent, with the working parent(s) benefiting from this dual involvement. Morally driven organizations, married and single adults can create implementation and methods of internal development. The elderly and parents involved would gain in a child's loving return, and a renewed sense of responsible living and energy.

There would be a reduction in the number of latchkey children entering a home that is normally empty and frightening to a child. The goal of the program is to benevolently alter people into becoming responsible adults who have been conditioned to develop, and then manage their individual destinies without government intervention.

By satellite and camera lens the current ecological health of the Earth can be presented with overlays to accommodate an environmental transition. The views from space over the past twenty-years show the rapid environmental and urban destruction we have generated during our lifetimes. From the pure blues and greens of our oceans and air to the deforestation of our rainforests the viewer can grasp the devastation we have caused. Then with this same process we can picture this planet five decades from now if nothing changes. With the proper presentations the audience would be able to grasp the Earth's pain and Her reactions, now represented by our climatic weather changes.

Using this same process in reverse we can then visualize a future world, the result of practical commonsense planning where cohabitation with the ecology is treated with respect and business enterprise. Mag-lev trains connected to monorail systems could be explained as a cost effective relief to our current highway systems and our insatiable thirst for oil, as an example. The responsible harvesting of fresh water with transference from areas of abundance to areas in drought, its storage and the development of underground energy and filtration systems (to include the replanting of the World's rainforest) could create high levels of sweat equity employment nationally and globally

New thinking could be implemented by combining all governmental social services to be gradually and sensitively transferred to the private sector over a period of five to twenty years. The outcome could be a transition and phase-in/out of all people programs to be implemented and managed through not-for-profit organizations, schools and inter-denominational churches, administrated with checks and balances incorporating government and media oversight to minimize personal abuse and business corruption.

A cost analysis of the savings long-term could be determined by taking the overhead of the present social programming (incorporating the costs of our prisons, education, law-enforcement and judicial processes etc.), and project the financial savings to answer the question of who is going to pay for the initial stages of this societal transference. If we know where our government leadership is taking us, America's corporate world could plan accordingly and save money and energy, minimize waste by knowing and planning for the overall objectives.

Our personal attitudes can be changed in each generational phase if people are shown where they are in the process, and how they will mutually benefit from their personal involvement. The past law-making methods, the ideologies, power seeking and conflict can be replaced with moral concern and benevolent caring for our personal families and this nation of ours.

Each of us has the potential of becoming sensitive to the different levels of our personal responsibilities to each other in this process. Simple things, like neighbor working with neighbor in reconstructing our inner cities (a larger scope and philosophy of Habitat for Humanity), with the option of ownership would re-establish pride of the neighborhood once again.

By incorporating vocational education into this equation, inner city persons can be educated to work together learning a trade, with all of us, on all socioeconomic levels, eventually becoming self-supportive and learning to exist with our many neighbors. In the process, each of us can learn to accept discipline and an evolving level of respect and moral ethics.

Through all of these introductions, the human spirit can become sensitive to how human emotions function, to just feel and communicate by being in each other's life in a constructive, civil manner. We could create, through our religious and educational institutions, a mode of positive interaction of establishing human bonding that is earned and not abused. To have each of us as God's children understand the lifetime commitments and the responsibilities that come with bringing a new soul onto this Earth.

We could re-establish trust by fulfilling one's promises with empathy, understanding, and compromising peacefully with each other in the transition. Children formally learning to not jump into the use of drugs or sexual or marital relationships without realizing what they were getting into. Each young soul could be brought to the recognition of the energies and commitment needed to raise a child, and the overall lifetime ramifications of their actions.

We could learn not to dwell on the bigotry, hatred and mistake making of our present and past. We could also rethink the human drain of our present way of doing things.

We can learn corporately that the demands on our lives have presented us with differing escalations and priorities requiring different levels of energy and talent. We can learn to peaceably act, tied in with the ability to obtain a well-paying job. To fall in love, with marriage lasting a lifetime. And to mentor our grandchildren and their grandchildren to better the system they will be inheriting from their parents.

As we are in our forth generation of family breakdowns producing uneducated parents who are siring more children adding to the cycle, there will be no quick fixes or easy solutions. It may take two to three generations of time to adjust future corrections. We will also have to explore and develop a consensus establishing long-term what we are willing to sacrifice short-term, to finance the entire process for the next three generations.

The underlying concept is to think two generations ahead in developing the future existence for our children's children — ad-infinitum. Creating an education and life conditioning which would enhance the second and developing third chapter of our nation's evolution. A future re-establishing the hopes and dreams we had when we were kids--just innocent children trying simply to grow up and be happy with our later lives.

****

Now place your mind into a period two decades from now. Consciously picture a small group of farsighted, common sense individuals working together to develop a strong, asset-use program of a pure working democracy, incorporating an on-going, 50-year plan for the Earth and its global populations. A concept publicly developed and marketed through the use of the media gaining widespread public support. The main motivation is the human anticipation of what the future holds in store.

Envision numerous small and Fortune 500 companies eventually repositioned from their past thinking, reversing short-term profit making into becoming good stewards of the Earth, structured for long-term gain. The business communities working in tandem with strategic non-profit government planning to address four specific areas of human change, to include environmental, political and social alterations through educational reform.

Through town meetings, using the media for information transference, a firm public consensus was constantly evolving in determining where we were going as a nation and digesting the outfalls of past "cause and effect". It was recognized that the past methods of making money via the industrial age polluted the environment and resulted in horrendous human erosion leading into a general anxiousness and socioeconomic divisions.

With the introduction of sociogenetics and information filtering systems, new user-friendly industry developed with the Earth being naturally restored. Each step creating an architectural code and a visionary outline, a road map developing the future outcome of who and what we wanted to become. The cities' and counties' populations, now teeming with healthy life forms, are the result of this positive interaction of man's intelligence. In essence, treating this spaceship we mutually are traveling on as one's personal home in a prudent and caring manner.

Production and manufacturing procedures were altered and streamlined, using clean energy for energy and propulsion. Hydrogen, fusion, fuel cells and the sun used as the primary resources along with wind and water. Farming methods were revolutionized with the use of pesticides, herbicides and other manmade poisons including polluting fertilizers minimized, and eventually discontinued, a period of phasing out the methods of non-organic and subsidized product manipulation.

There were now wide applications of organic farming initiated, and low energy precision applications of moisture, creating new industry, and jobs, paying livable incomes for the citizens of the United States and the balance of the world's populations. This transference was initially underwritten with short-term, 20-year, government tax incentives and subsidies to initiate acceptance with matching financial facility from the private sector.

Utmost consideration was given to protecting the composition of our planet concentrating on renewable resources allowing for the transitions, utilizing this country's space and archeological programs. Bio-intensive agricultural methods were introduced with crops grown in a circular fashion, with the market value increasing with each new season's production. The concrete and asphalt highways of the late 20th century were replaced with monorail systems interlocked with high-speed rail for transportation services. This, in turn, reduced waste-runoff and the nation's dependency on the combustible engine and oil. The median strips of once worn-out interstate systems now support underground fiber-optic utility lines and aqueducts for energy transference and water.

Throughout each community and nationwide, persons from the private sector worked with local high schools, colleges, universities and vocational institutions to educate, train and retrain people. Middle-class jobs were being restored with planned cottage industries developing clean production methods of restoring the Earth. The primary thrust: To stay focused to educate minds through projections of anticipated need. The inner spirit and human energies of the nation's cities and urban life were being renewed in this transformation, with personal self-esteem taking precedence over human despondency.

Planning and zoning departments on the local level worked with the business communities, social organizations, educational, environmental and social architects making far-reaching decisions of what would and could be developed creating a comprehensive social reorganization and land-use plan. Human services and property values were naturally improved from this intelligent process of non-political and bi-partisan applications of using the best-devised programs gleaned throughout the world.

A business plan with cash-flow management incorporated an operating budget that was formally initiated and approved by the public at large. The prudent implementation of social program privatization resulted in government downsizing and lessened the need for political input. This transformation eliminated the duplication of services, and the expensive waste of money and talented personnel, a process initiated privately and publicly to repair the past damage of our abuses nationwide.

By envisioning the middle of the 21st century, a modern-day Pentagon was duplicated to develop human change, linked regionally and nationally utilizing the structures of antiquated military bases throughout the world. This electronically-linked complex acted as a collecting magnet and information clearing house, poised for the utilization of man's thoughts and idea making, with effective implementation.

By analyzing the history and cause of each problem, practical applications for human reprogramming were developed. The facility, structured to analyze cause and effect, tied in the nation's schools and libraries worldwide through a global web of telecommunications. Individuals with common sense applications and working experience were fulfilling the roles of social and economic architects and engineers.

It was understood that there were many programs and ideas working in local communities and worldwide, which could be learned from, and incorporated into a national consensus. People working with people to peacefully develop the strategies and long-term focus, with sensitive intelligence and planning. It was also anticipated that there would be a human reluctance in creating human benevolence and compassion.

It was also recognized that in the early 2000s more than two-thirds of the domestic population received some form of government dole. Each person in this number conditioned to receive with little effort and adamant about not giving up one's entitlements. There were numerous old-guard factions of special interests protecting their turfs, attempting to dilute any major possibility for real change, which would continually need to be addressed.

It was realized that government practices on all levels were caught up in a quagmire of nepotism, cronyism, corruption and personal academic failure with the educational systems doing the same. Our mutated form of manipulative economic forces and class separation of the previous century had become a major cause of division and social failure. The past responsibilities and objectives of our government were ill defined and improperly managed, not focused or visionary in their structure. As a result, looking at the larger picture, our competing for immediate profit and return on investment created a school of human piranha that were feeding on the carcass of the United States.

It was realized that the public's environmental concerns had evolved into adversarial individualistic agendas instead of creating a willingness to have all factions find a common ground and work together. That the motivations of government agencies and business profiteering flew in the face of the many ecological groups in trying to preserve and restore the fragile balance of the Earth. The intuitive common sense inner workings of each person making the decisions for each of these factors had become suppressed and defensive, with a line drawn in the sand. Most, if not all, expressing a personal concern in their own way, yet destroying what they were trying to save.

The moral fiber and fabric of this country realized, during this period, that to institute change takes the insight and resources of the entire country working together, developing alterations to fix what was then breaking. A forum and corporate picture was presented to the American public addressing each class of problems with proposed solutions, outlining their strengths and weaknesses with their short and long-term obligations and financial costs identified. All programs that were working locally, regionally and worldwide were placed into an informational pool to be continually analyzed as to their effectiveness in this reformation. That for any human to succeed in developing vision and successful programming must operate outside, then inside, the political spectrum to be long lasting and effective.

Public meetings were scheduled to solicit all public opinion discussing the various options, and to grasp the overall cause and effect of each situation. It was understood that there was a tremendous need for each participant to understand where one is coming from (to undercut hidden agendas and inexperience), with a sensitivity that can only come from walking in the shoes of those currently affected. This led into a continual open discussion with each social program's history examined as to its overall human effectiveness. Each program's future would be re-engineered then mandated via public debate and the voting booth.

Backed by public consensus, utilizing the television and the information highway of the Internet, the President with Congress, then politically mandated a step-by-step process managing the overhaul. Through political committee and public debate, several paths were elected through the democratic processes at the polls by geographic regions. This developed into simplified and easily understood ecological reprogramming to be governed with a master plan for national implementation, utilizing the United Nations for later global management.

It was realized that all persons on all fronts had to be similarly affected, paying a mutual price. The vehicle was a picture of what the short-term costs would be while explaining the long-range goals and their human savings. In essence, creating mutual sweat equity for anticipated mutual results, minimizing fear and personal positioning. Each government in turn regionalized the recommendations for study and local revision.

Taking the best the world and each locale had to offer; all working options in all human areas were analyzed, and then modified for regional and local applications. The initial platform led into test programs of 3-5 year durations for monitoring then assessing the results, using the private sector for guidance and implementation on a regional, then national basis. After fine-tuning the after effects, business plans with operating budgets were developed for long-term national introductions.

The goal of national and eventually global applications was to be entertained with each success and failure monitored, with each region supplying the information and energies for a continual modification. The world's public was educated to realize that it would be far better to plan for the future, than to randomly allow it to happen by accident. They, in turn, would learn over several generations to embrace this concept to create an affordable future if all people would mutually benefit by working and sacrificing together. The motivation was economics and the human internal drive of competition, supplying quality services with lowered prices as the end product.

Education, social programs re-establishing the family unit including affordable medical care, and ecological protection were given the highest priority. This allowed each person to be responsible for creating his or her personal destiny. Persons were in a constant mode of being educated via the written media, radio, movies and TV, creating demand for new industries and joint-venture enterprises. The world's best existing and most cost-effective programs in each social area were introduced in unison, one in each region for analysis and monitoring for their effectiveness.

Initially the phase-in, phase-out concept for the United States was financed with private grants, and matching federal facility for the first 20 to 50 years, then reverted to 100% privatization. Through economic competition, general operations and governmental social agencies' programs became affordable, cost effective and user friendly. Contracts were awarded by open bid, determined by the common sense of the text, and the working experience of individuals.

The wastefulness of social and bureaucratic managed programs duplication was eliminated, saving billions of dollars in federal spending. With the nation's financial overhead prudently managed, this inventive path allowed a deflationary monetary stance, reducing the principal indebtedness of the country. Basic services became less costly (motivated by competitive financial pressures), eventually lowering the personal tax base. This objective provided the general motivation for personal acceptance and voluntary approval of becoming an income tax free state.

Through the printed and screen news-media resources, a list of altruistic, reputable, knowledgeable and sensitive persons and organizations were recruited from their local successes to populate the complexes. Each individual and group expressed a willingness to pool their abilities in developing an architectural design for the planet and its populations, leaving one's ego and pride outside the doors. Common sense, down-to-earth people fulfilled the responsibilities as mentors to educate others, and to show how to implement each step for local applications.

Students, parents and teachers can mutually create lifetime programs for their individual evolution. To incorporate what worked from their experiences and hearts and minds to create a single umbrella approach for our nation's inner repair. An integrated system initiated to identify individual gifts and talents, leaving the mind with the ability to create and to think logically, developing a master concept. The responsibilities of parenting and adult involvement were constantly stressed. This effort incorporated the use of the electronic media and thousands of experienced, moral persons for information transference and implementation.

Town meetings were being constantly conducted with key concerns presented on a continual basis for simplified explanation and nurturing. A picture and path devised with all persons traveling the same path, working together in tandem. Altruistic human beings with a clear idea of the steps and mutual time frame developed using an integrated style of management.

Using screen technology, satellite and computer with total people involvement, the pieces of the puzzle are shaped with each region and local community developing the picture together. The objective a collection of shared experiences and theory as an architect and general contractor would design a building's construction. A well-managed operation attracting this country's best and brightest, working with persons involved on the street with common sense applications finally surfacing.

The effort and energies include provisions for constant adjustment, never losing sight of the goals and objectives re-establishing a strong, involved middle-class America. Allowing him and her and their children the human possibility of creating their own answers. The key and driving vista was to give the common man a chance once again, and to approach many of our social problems areas in tandem, with the same energy and efficiency through a collective focus.

CHAPTER XV
THIS SPACESHIP EARTH

Somehow, somewhere, it all began 4 1/2 billion years ago. Whether it was from the angiosperms falling from the heavens or the ebbs and flows of the universe's internal forces, this planet's existence is overwhelming in its majesty and synergistic balance, created with the capacity to support all life forms.

Our astronauts in their numerous excursions into space have found themselves emotionally and mentally overwhelmed with the intricate vastness surrounding the fragile existence of this Earth. Surveying a sunrise and sunset, more than eighteen times a day, while drifting in orbit, is nothing less than a totally surreal sensation of an endless harmony. The meshing of land and sea, sky and Earth and the stars in the heavens are an ultimate involvement with our God and the Universe, and our special home. Our human capabilities have yet to evolve with the sensitivity to grasp what our psyche's feel, other than just being overwhelmed.

To view a hurricane forming, growing into a gigantic mushroom, and then pounding the Earth's surface has to be an ultimate experience not only from within, but with the Creator of All. NASA's many voyages and our times have yet to produce the vision that adequately describes this truly humbling life experiment, for if it did, we would stop doing what we are doing to this home.

We are moving in a spiraling frenzy creating a picture of a future environment we are definitely uneducated to comprehend. We are exploring with the unknown worlds generating new challenges, as this planet's integrity is overly stressed and now negatively reactive.

Instead of arguing the pros and cons of the facts or having a hidden agenda requiring more study, we will have to learn to get our act together, to take care of what we have done to ourselves with a global sense of urgency. This Earth is screaming in pain.

From coast to coast to the vistas pictured worldwide, we can sense with our eyes our not using the Earth's assets wisely. When nature strikes out and back with a vengeance, she is crying out as a child wanting us to pay attention and listen.

There are growing numbers of people who believe that this planet is a living entity, a self-contained and total regenerating spaceship. That all of life and the inner workings of this Earth are intricately intertwined and interdependent upon the other, feeding off larger reproductive balances that our Creator provides.

We can compare this, on a differing scale, to the human body with its reproductive atoms and cells working together in tandem to keep us alive and functioning. When our skin of the body is cut, burned or it's internal organs struck with a parasite or wound, the healing internal mechanisms of our anatomy come into play aided by interior scientific forces. The antibodies, the white and red blood cells, act as a scalpel attacking the root cause of the problem allowing the body to experience a transition and an internal healing.

Our Earth with its larger dynamics addresses her infections and pains similar to our human processes with a self-diagnosis coming into play. She focuses on her restoration through earthquakes, volcanoes, fires, drought, windstorms and flooding, cleansing and surgically addressing her traumas away. When a doctor or nurse punctures our skin with a needle to draw blood, it would be comparable to our hydrocarbon industries drilling the Earth's surface for oil, draining some of the planet's healing properties. Or the private business sector clear cutting old growth forest for habitation and profit would be comparable to shaving the Earth's epidermis with a dull razor blade.

The pores, the different layers of the human processes, even the tears from one's eyes could be compared to the lands and lubricating properties of our oils, soils, oceans and seas. When mankind's abuse exceeds certain levels the Earth strikes back with a vengeance for repair, for the more severe the damage, the more severe the cure. Ten of the most devastating environmental disasters ever recorded in our modern times, have happened in the last decade, with global weather extremes escalating in intensity and destructiveness.

Today our ecological and economic world is made of three distinct groups of persons leading into wasteful confrontations of wasted energies leading into our most severe ecological disasters. Diverse and differently motivated people who see the world through their own agendas and individualized interpretations creating their own corporate priorities.

On one side reside environmental extremists, who are labeled "bunny and tree huggers", who do not want to see anything abused at all. These persons believe that all life is inner-related with the intuitive instinct to co-exist with total interdependence on the other. That even a blade of grass should not be cut or touched, as nature and man get thrown out of balance with its loss.

On the completely opposite side of the spectrum is the opportunist driven by money and the need to develop by any means. The thinking and driving force is that it is a capitalistic right to clear cut old growth forest or fish out the lakes and oceans using our God given ingenuity. That it makes good economic sense to dump the chemical aftermath of our manufacturing life styles into the air, ground or our seas to add to a company's bottom line. They support the political mentality to keep environmental programs and causes at bay and in constant feasibility study.

The people in this number personally believe that it is mankind's "right" to use this spaceship any way we can; there is too much profit to be made by not doing otherwise. Out of sight translates to out of mind; "we" don't have to be responsible for our short-term actions and abuses, morally removing themselves from our human responsibilities of being good stewards of this Earth. They believe that nature has accommodated man's exploits in the past and that, somehow or other, things will work out all right in the end.

The third group consists of many different sensitivities and beliefs, with differing layers of human concern attempting to accommodate these two extremes. This segment of individuals realizes that it is difficult for these two mentalities to understand that our economic health is also interdependent on the ecological integrity of this planet, Earth. They attempt to arbitrate the many differing shades of gray with logical fact and thought but, in growing instances, lose this option to the moneyed interests who control politics and its political decisions.

Our present methodologies of governing ourselves in this democracy, driven by capitalism and now global greed, have made it most difficult to be fair to this planet and us. Capitalistic thinking allows the rights of the businessman and property owner to take precedence over the needs of the "community at large" overwhelming the intricate balancing act that nature provides.

Because of money, power and the corruptions of financial and political control, our mind sets and attention spans are played upon, keeping us humanly separated from coexisting within the actual energies of this planet. A small handful of our common neighbors driven to protect what they think they own, manipulate our larger corporate decisions, decisions that have now created a true possibility of this planet self-destructing.

There are many voices that present a platform for common sense ecological balance that also find themselves locked in wasteful combat with these moneyed forces. Their voices and warnings become mocked and convoluted, displaced with politics requiring more study. Our human intuitiveness is ignored, with smokescreens and economic diversions then playing upon the emotions of the public. Out of this, we continually move backwards as a human society, duplicating our continual errors by allowing history to negatively replicate itself. The Earth is now being held to a ransom to benefit but a handful of people with their need for more wealth, more than they will ever be able to spend in their lifetimes.

Our personal feelings and concern in this matter are offset by our human natures, as personal fears of job loss and probable tax increases are emotionally played upon. For this reason, the moneyed thinking is that it is best to keep our internal processes where they are, making ecological changes difficult, if near impossible, to assimilate what this planet can support.

By satellite, we see the changes of the Earth's condition over the past 40 years driven by our industrial age, and our age of greed. Using visual technology and computer imaging we are able to create evolutionary portrayals of our planet since the beginning of its time. With satellite and camera lens circling our globe, we can now experience what we have accomplished, the damage we have inflicted upon this fragile balance of life.

What used to be beautiful colors of brilliance just two decades ago have been transformed into dull grays, orange and brown hues. From the Hugo and Andrew hurricanes to the flooding, tornado and hail damage in the Mid and Far West and the South, with increasing levels of drought and fire damage nationwide, God and nature are trying to tell us something. We are not listening well.

In this land blessed with naturally abundant drinking water, we are purchasing this bottled liquid at 90 cents a gallon and more, because of our personal doubts about the quality of our local resources. Overpopulation, economic disparity and greed are accelerating the demise of our old growth and rain forest creating the Earth's desertification, which when combined with all of the above, are disabling the planet's internal processes of regeneration.

When we give thought to the basics of "cause and effect" we can come to the realization that we have flooding and drought because the green space absorbing qualities of our open space have been displaced by man's current methods of building and harvesting product. In maintaining our current lifestyles each of our cities produces heavy metals and oil residues from our concrete and asphalt existence creating thermal barriers into the stratosphere, affecting moisture patterns. Our once fertile farmlands that act as sponges and filtration systems, when lost to development are soon replaced by non-absorbing concrete and asphalt, which accelerates erosion and the concentration of our waste by-products.

Our sewage and garbage systems produce nitrogen, methane and other toxic gases, with atomic sludge added to the waste pool. Our industry emissions produce chemical effluent percolating into our oceans and lakes creating deformed reptiles and fish, and mutant waters filled with algae, viruses and unknown toxins. Our construction sites produce sediments that are blended into the effluent produced by these and other polluting sources. The ingredients then mix with the manure, pesticides and fertilizers used to produce our nation's food supply. Urban sprawl then adds bacteria and virus from its inefficient sewer treatment systems with the underground water resources we drink and the air we breathe absorbing the entire combination of these discharges.

The natural disasters we experience, which are nature's way of evolving and giving herself a bath are being accelerated today, because of the by-products of what we extract and dispense. We populate areas that are prone to flooding, fires and earthquake, or being swept by high winds because of our indifference and lack of sensitivity, ignoring the practical sense of cohabitating with this world on which we live.

We are now faced with a growing collective unknown, as few political minds can grasp the collective damage, as our nest is truly fouled and increasingly deadly to us all. There are a growing number of doctors, eco-scientists and we, the general public, who suspect that our increasing numbers of terminal illnesses, including the advancing and increasing early stages of our cancers, the re-emergence of old diseases of smallpox, malaria and hepatitis, are becoming accelerated by our being surrounded by and ingesting our own waste. The result is an increase in the number of persons developing reproductive problems and immune/respiratory problems, to include AID's and antibiotic resistant viruses and bacteria shortening our global life spans.

A few toxic elements, in themselves, may create little physical damage, as we have fairly resilient defense mechanisms, but combined we have a major, collective cesspool on our hands. The waters we now drink, the air we breathe and the foods we eat universally are in a silent, but deadly combustion into themselves. The current result is the repetitive and expensive effects of massive rodent infestations, acid rain with a growing hole in our ozone, now jeopardizing our food chain.

One hundred years ago, less than one out of ten of us would die from cancer or an early heart attack. Today, one out of three of us are dying prematurely from our exposures to these chemical combinations, all similar to the historical foundations and the re-creation of the "Black Plague" of Europe nine hundred years ago.

Now with the "greenhouse effect", the cause still heavily debated but gaining our attention (because of our dramatic weather changes nationally and worldwide) we have a global catastrophe on our hands. A deadly human challenge of earthly proportions, initiated during our lifetimes that will require all of us to alter our current lifestyles.

****

In the late 1800s the driving force of business development was hindered by a global economic recession. Although not planned for, this malaise generated a new era, tying in human ingenuity with vision and personal risk-taking. A handful of persons motivated by poverty and their personal problems inadvertently created new thinking benefiting the world for well over one hundred years. The Fords, Astors, Mellons and Rockefellers et al enterprises created new opportunity for man, driven by their individual hunger and thirst and their inquisitive natures. Because of their individual vision, taking chances and utilizing their ingenuity they also developed our current global ecological abuse creating our dependence on, and the need for the combustion engine with its insatiable thirst for oil.

Life and living on this planet is one of the most fragile balancing acts we have as human mortals. Comparable perhaps, but on a much larger scale, to the vulnerabilities and pains of an adolescent simply growing up. The complex, integrated energies of this planet are not easily pictured or verbally defined for one to easily understand, which is the reason for comparing it to the natural functions of the human body.

It is not politically palatable to accept the need to re-prioritize, then adjust our way of life to accommodate the environmental needs of the Earth without a major rethinking of what we have that surrounds us. To put this in perspective, we should realize that less than 3% of all water in and on this Earth is considered fresh and drinkable. Eighty-seven percent of this "three percent" number is frozen or toxically contaminated by human production. It is thought that every forty years or so, that each drop of water returns to the point where it started. With 6.2 billion people now needing to mutually use this resource, we have altered this method of recycling, this kidney filtration capacity with our consumption and waste.

In its travels, this liquid goes from fresh to salt and collects and digests molecules in its travels. We dump thousand of tons of our industrial by-product annually into our oceans, rivers and streams while it is moving. The significance is that if we lose our planet's integrity and its ability to balance what we are doing, that everything else — power, control, manipulation and our economic well-being is going to be a moot point.

According to United Nation population projections human growth will increase 50% in the next four decades adding additional stress on the worlds' existing supplies of fresh water. One billion, two hundred million people in the world presently do not have access to potable resources. By 2050 almost seven billion people will be faced with water scarcity. In the United States, right now, over 40% of our water bodies are no longer safe for human use. We will have nowhere else to hide.

It is best to accept that this planet is the only one we've got and there is no vault with a cover big enough to protect us; there is nowhere else safe to relocate. And to the moneyed, controlling interests who are doing the damage, to realize and grasp the knowledge that no one to date has figured how to take any of their wealth gained with them when they are dead.

Today, our domestic political leadership addresses this situation with lip service, politically demanding additional feasibility studies ignoring the root cause of the problem; the problems well identified by the U.N. sponsored "findings meetings" in Johannesburg, South Africa, Montreal, Rio de Janeiro, and Kyoto, Japan. From the many conclusions drawn from our ecological experts, there is now an overwhelming acceptance by the rest of the world in recognizing that we are in the process of ecologically destroying ourselves, and this planet supporting our travels.

Because of scientific fact, many world's leaders, eco-scientists and engineers are generating a dramatic first step with recommendations and programs to address our many ecological ills. All common sense approaches underwritten by the rest of the world to date are ignored by the politics and economics of the United States. Our common sense values are being negated by but a handful of us motivated by our corporate mentality of entitlements, a secularized mentality, which arrogantly and belligerently believes that we have too much to lose — financially.

****

Throughout the early to mid 1900s, an ecological vista for this country was developed but lost in the throes of war and world depression. The messages of Thoreau, Leopold and a Benton MacKaye (forester, author, philosopher), and a handful of their later contemporaries, including scientists Cousteau and Sagan, introduced their concepts and concerns for the nation's and the world's ecology.

Benton MacKaye, a visionary thinker, created a picture and road map in his mind to promote wilderness preservation and a greening of our nation. He believed that through man's human spirit a possible cohabitation with this world could be sensibly implemented that human development could be accommodated in a much larger vista by planning for the long-term. The concept envisions a harmonious blending of man's interaction that would also enhance our country's natural resources. Buildings and concrete construction are visualized to utilize the terrains, the rolling plains, mountains and seas with a blending development of man's use of sweat equity and intelligence.

The little known book, *The New Exploration*, initiated a movement to rethink the massive damage and high costs of unplanned development growth and the human stresses created by not anticipating the outcome. The concept evolved into an informal clearinghouse for new ecological thinking incorporating the necessary steps for land reclamation, flood control, energy utilization, a reforestation program and how we use our roads. To utilize the land and the Earth in a way that the inhabitants would become responsible stewards of what was originally offered.

The major accomplishment of this initial effort resulted in the formation of the Appalachian Trail. The first 2,000 mile hiking path linking Maine to Georgia, in the American Continent, and our current park systems philosophy embraced by President Theodore Roosevelt. Today, what we have is far removed from the scope of what was then envisioned, again because of our nearsightedness and our self-created secular divisions. Our present towns and major cities interspersed with nature's natural beauty and balance from this harmonious introduction were lost to other political priorities and our capitalistic need to acquire money at any cost.

It is for this reason that a cumulative concept and overview for the Earth's health has been developed under the auspices of the world's United Nations. The best and brightest of our environmental world have taken the pieces and developed a long-range, multi-step plan for man's co-existence with this globe.

Many of our world scientists and eco-engineers are now recognizing that our oceans, seas and forests worldwide produce over 99.9% of our oxygen, and that we are now experiencing climatic change as a result of our over development, population growth and abusive lifestyles. While not all are embracing the causes of impending weather and storm changes or human starvation as being accelerated by our abuse, the general public and many of our world leaders are now spiritually and secularly opened to recognize the need for dramatic change.

The initial provision is for the development of an international agreement on specific measurements to protect our air and the interrelated diversity of all living things. This overview includes the need to maintain our old growth forest, our oceans and seas with practical application of industrial balance.

In this line of thinking, if sensitive educational programming and financial rewards had been thoughtfully placed in the birthing control processes of each culture, there would be less need to produce the number of children who are prematurely dying. If the wood-dependent industries worldwide worked with vision and had replanted hardwoods and recycled what they cut years ago, there would not be the shortage of virgin forests presently. If Madison Avenue in its marketing schemes had stressed less paper packaging for product sales there would have been less stress on nature's replenishing herself, and more jobs generated from this form of anticipatory investing.

It has been proven by environmental accounting methods that an acre of rain forest left to naturally replenish itself is worth over $3800 in renewable materials, which is a fortune in the Second and Third Worlds. Still to be found are the intricate balances of all that our Father provides. Be it a simple remedy for a future disease, or a national park attracting tourists, general future planning and prudent common sense thinking can generate hard currency for the host nations. It is because of this thought process a second step has been created consisting of a global Earth Charter for all countries and their collective populations. This provision creates a picture of what the planet and each region can support while establishing moral stewardship for resource preservation and restoration.

It is a detailed economic and environmental plan and the initial step of understanding the costs of our non-cohesive human interaction. An Agenda 21 concept incorporating the current pieces and challenges creating a comprehensive one hundred year plan for this Earth of God's and our future human survival.

United Nations' personnel and other experienced specialists are in the position to supply the technological guidance and formula funding to produce a positive outcome and picture. The concept lays out a step-by-step assimilation including the operational costs, human changes and education needed for worldwide applications. Yet, there are certain individuals, including the United States, who do not want to accept the initial alterations of their comfort zones losing their political control.

As this book is about personal spiritual growth to induce social change, taking off our rose colored glasses and thinking in a practical manner, we have to recognize that we have been ill educated to embrace the concept of personal preservation. We have inadvertently evolved into a nation believing that what we are doing is mostly correct, not understanding the much larger political vista. Our domestic leadership is reluctant to retrofit or pay for any environmental accommodation, as the total truth would create their future unemployment and legal action for incompetence by the public at large.

We will soon be forced to conclude that our economic vitality is tied to the integrity of the Earth, and that our future is dependent upon how quickly we adapt to this thinking. As we can well understand money, the economics of environmental repair are accelerating in their intensity and number and in the near future will become a political and personal nightmare. The insurance industry, which dwarfs all others, is now escalating its cost to do business to a level which will no longer be affordable, similar to the medical profession attempting to control the explosive operating costs addressing the needs of an aging and polluted population but on a much larger global scale.

If we and the political community are shown how we can get from point A to point B for less long range expense, moving us out of this age of industrialization into a cleaner age of production, each person can learn to embrace the concept for intelligent change for the ecology and save money in the process. When our business and government leaders evolve in their profit and loss thinking, conservation and recycling can be market driven, doing away with our dependence on the combustion engine and its need for oil. By encouraging the business sector to develop a customer base for the waste by-product before it is produced, this small initial step can save hundreds of billions of dollars each year. The goal could be a mutually developed process of financial rewards and tax punishments to develop services and goods with less waste products and the use of fuel.

The "Earth Share" programs in the United States and the "Greens Movement" in Europe and the ecological programs of Costa Rica and Japan presently have numerous programs in place that are saving its private business sector that could be replicated with "tinkered" improvement. There are tax and profit incentives to produce more, using less. We could come to the realization that our throwaway mentality has resulted in a nation wasting over 700 billion dollars annually in energy use, overwhelming the quality of our air and our landfills. Our technology is still in its infancy in developing sea power, biomass, fiberoptic transference, solar and other renewable energy sources including hydrogen and could generate jobs and new industries similar to our recent decade of the Internet/.Com era, globally.

From imaging developed almost 100 years ago, we can grasp the concept of a national greening of our country and eventually the rest of the world. We can rethink how we develop and orchestrate this upcoming 21st century of ours. Our current bicycle and hiking paths, jogging trails and traveling systems can be incorporated into a national concept creating human harmony and peaceful interaction. The land's integrity, the flow of water, the flooding and drought cycles can be accommodated by the records of history and planning.

The development and restoration of our old and new cities can be a rethinking of what we want to look at and how we want to live with the Earth. Sports Meccas could be envisioned with supporting cottage industries encouraged, not only in this country but also throughout this world. Rural agricultural areas could be transformed into a patchwork quilt of different shades of dirt and leaf. Drip irrigation could be phased in to intelligently conserve high-level use of water. Our country and our cities could be planned out as a giant golf course, less the use of chemicals in its production, incorporating the ecological future of man.

Through the development of massive underground aqueducts constructed to transfer and feed local reservoirs for water storage and usage, we could eliminate many of the problems of flooding and shortages during the periods of drought. Those regions being flooded could be the source of this liquid gold to areas in need and vise-versa, paid for by those who use the water. This project could be incorporated into a national railway system on the magnitude of our nations interstate highway system of the 1950s and financed by the savings of increased productivity and phasing out our highway and utilities maintenance funding.

Our suburban and urban planners could incorporate more green space and rooftop gardens emulating our local, state and national park systems. Present cities concrete and asphalt "hot houses" would be interspersed with parks and gardens improving the attitudes of the inhabiting people. A person looking down on the landscape would view a pristine quilt of man and nature harmoniously working together as one.

Low usage numbers and the lack of alternative timely systems presently hamper mass transit. A future rail system could be transformed into slow and high-speed transport, incorporating natural renewable energy forms, supplemented by solar-propelled and natural hydrogen-gas bus systems. Increased usage could be phased-in by a plan of odd and even car license numbering to alleviate human resistance. The traffic on our current road systems would theoretically be cut in half.

We would need fewer highways and could concentrate development into high-density areas eliminating the sprawl and congestion of our suburbia and use less oil. This would then allow the nation's communities to consolidate and incorporate services, lowering their general overhead costs and in turn manage growth through concurrency. What this means is that all infrastructure including roads, utilities and their related support systems, schools and all public services would be in place before approving any additional development.

We have the technology in our classrooms, laboratories and corporate worlds to correct our garbage generation and accelerate the decaying processes. With the introduction of biotech methods we can destroy much of our refuse problems with natural organic, safe biogenetic materials. We can restore our landfills' properties and reprocess our polluted waters with osmosis filtering with organic bacterial applications. By incorporating our current theory with current and new technology we can reduce our viral problems with non-intrusive bacteria safely devouring their residues in the process of cleansing.

Utilizing today's research methods, talent and monies can be invested to benefit the community at large by developing an after market for the waste produced before it is generated. Our oil and utility conglomerates could invest in long-range funding and research pools with a number of joint capital investments motivated by long-range planned profit and future opportunity.

Once business and government have established a mutual vision, a picture describing what it is going to do and where it is going would lead into our future ecological transformation adding future business planning. Transportation, manufacturing, our medical and chemical industries could develop new sciences and practices to reprocess and reduce what they create. These new industries and resources created in-house and sold through innovative new marketing methods on Wall Street will result in new diversified account base with profit additions to the financial bottom line.

The persons who can inject an "immediacy mentality" for environmental rescue are sitting in the offices of our corporate and political worlds. These persons will need to be shown how to profit short-range, by financially co-existing with this planet we're mutually traveling for the long-term.

CHAPTER XVI
MONEY, POLITICS AND US

The Persians developed the coin system before the time of the Greek Empires during the era of 3100 B.C. It is believed that they had tired of using plant products and livestock as barter, a cumbersome method of exchange. Approximately 3,000 years later, Augustus Caesar became the first living face to appear on a gold coin, elevating himself to the status of a living God. In 250 A.D. the precious metal content in each of these coins was cut down to 40%, which caused a mid level period of inflation. Twenty years later, the valued content was bled to 4% resulting in a temporary failure of the Roman Banking system.

About this same time, a new coin was issued by the Aurelian Empire, which was backed by the value of the bounty and conquests of the East. The value of these coins was artificially increased 2 ½ times hoping to stay ahead of inflation, but instead, resulted in prices soaring and a major rebellion of the working class. The Aurelian's army in defending the misguided decisions of their leadership incurred over 7,000 casualties.

The following losses to the civilian population were horrendous, caused by the ill-conceived monetary manipulations of its leadership's shortsighted intervention. As history is a consistent teacher, most wars have been fought, empires struck down, and man's good intentions for improving his lot in life are constantly set back, simply because of man's ego and self-manipulated greed.

The scholastic theme for our generation was similar to theirs, just different eras. Go out into the world, make money and then spend it. We, like they, were led to believe that we were invincible; that our leadership would make the proper decisions for us. That we would be able to accomplish all that we wanted and it would be accomplished within an affordable budget.

Today's political difficulties set in when we embraced this concept of having it "all" through the "American Dream", embraced with a personal passion and innocent blindness at the time. Looking back, with the benefit of this historical insight, it was also a period of our personal naiveté in accepting the commercial path that our leadership provided. Although we would like to believe that we in America have a multiparty political system built by a democracy, it is now an elephant and a donkey that are leading us into our current albatross and political disasters.

Today, most persons who have excessive amounts money and power seem to be obsessed about not losing what they have. They will oftentimes go to excessive lengths to protect the world in which they live. Many in this number live in walled fortresses and ivory palaces far removed from the many masses of people who have far less. Human nature being what it is, they really don't have the time to be personally bothered with anyone else's trials and tribulations. They have their piece of pie and their slice of America. For this small privileged group it is easier to let someone else be involved with the world's social and environmental problems, and have come to expect others to weather the storms of their personal indifference.

There are six methods of obtaining money for personal use. There are those who "work" hard to earn what they possess, and "invest" and "save" it wisely. There are others who "marry" into it, and others who "inherit" it from the labor of their parents and other loved ones, or profit from the utilization of the resources located where they reside. Then there is a much smaller number in this same profile that has "taken advantage of a situation" and then "took" to the greater expense of others. In the process they compromised the integrity of their existence, having leveraged the ability to listen to the morality and common sense contained within one's inner soul. This process of "stealing" corrupts the individual as the outcome, blinded to what they have become.

If you accept this premise to change how we are doing things, you will also realize that we will have to start conceptualizing ideas and programs outside our current human limitations. In essence, become more intimately aware of the larger responsibilities that each of us has in dealing with the immediate needs of God's world. Today the events of our times are crying out to us in a warning. What we do with these messages only time will tell, as we live in a society that is money driven.

Today, wealth and greed have so permeated our lives in America that is difficult to see beyond this wall of money in developing a future with less politics and human pain. The future will require that each of us voluntarily reengineer the importance of money as our prime motivator. All of the steps suggested to date will require a more benevolent and giving attitude. Only with this secularized change can a more spiritually driven world be derived.

There is a rising undercurrent of equalization in these times, perhaps induced by God's checks and balances on this capitalistic society and man's personal need for financial survival. Stock and business values have dropped considerably over the past few years, which is leveling the playing field. More persons who were financially removed from the realities of the common man are now being struck with a mutual fear that is crossing all socioeconomic levels.

Since the 11th of September, corporate America has hemorrhaged with bankruptcies and unemployment numbers at all time highs. Persons who were accustomed to living the high-life are now being brought to their knees facing a new economic reality. In this, we as a human race are learning that no matter how much we have, or how secure we may feel, that money can be lost too quickly, at any time, to some unknown force and entity. For this reason, all that is and will be suggested is to have us think internally in larger terms; reevaluating our personal and political priorities.

All that is proposed will require thinking outside our man-made boxes of space and time, as our current thinking will have to be short-circuited with our intuitive beliefs systems resurfacing. We will need to focus on a higher vista, while not shortcutting the operational procedures being suggested. And, if God is not in this picture, we will be historically recycling what we have done, as our governing structure is now the largest employer in the world.

We should realize that our federal government is a social experiment for us, with an annual budget of 3.4 trillion dollars at this writing. A governing body originally devised "for and by the people" is now far removed from the intentions of our nation's founders. Our socialize monster leading us is now our surrogate parent.

We presently have several options to address our current political situation. One is to do nothing keeping things the same. Two would be to put our heads under our pillows, hoping that God will intervene. Or three, we recognize the responsibilities that we have living in a democracy, and will do something positive with our lives. With this said, the following words provide several options for point three, that have the potential for developing future political change.

Because of the combative and nasty forces of politics demands in being elected or re-elected, each person elected, for many personal reasons, becomes jaundiced and far removed from being a true servant of the average American. Each human being who enters into this fray with the best of intentions is exposed to the inner workings of deal making, and is then corrupted by our current political and electoral system.

Once in a seat of legislative authority, and at each decision-making juncture, our politician's agendas become distorted by having to deal away part of the integrity that got them elected in the first place. Human nature being what it is, they evolve into believing in their self-entitlements and self-importance. In this, they become jaundiced and far removed from just being human.

The political world today process shreds one's ethics, and then conditions that individual to place themselves above those who permitted them office and decision-making power. With their perceive need to hold on to what they have become, with the need to acquire more at the expense to America at large, they become oblivious to the destruction being accomplished with their actions.

Wanting to become elected or reelected, politicians express a public level of personal concern while politically they are compromised through their political parties' agendas of wanting partisan control. After a period of several months or years this conditioning soon has them shaking their heads in disdain, personally removed from the concerns and plight of most others. A small handful then becomes dependent on the financial support of the corporations and their lobbyists who expect a substantial return on their investment. The politician then becomes the puppet for these moneyed interests.

Philosophically, we weather the many personal storms for our individual survival and advance through technological and educational inroads in fits and starts. We improve our standard of living through innovation and become willing to go to war to defend what we then possess. We then become distracted and lose our sense of purpose, with history repeating the process over and over again. We are now experiencing a same remake of historical proportions in that we have now fallen into the same repetitive dangers of all of our predecessors; with the likely chance to implode from within — all caused by money and politics and losing our spiritual focus.

Our founding fathers' major concern was a central governing body evolving out of the control of the people that it was designed to protect and govern. Their visionary concern is now fact. A handful of businessmen and their insider political connections are now involved in creating our nation's domestic policy and our current global direction. This will someday have to be reversed by us, as they are inadvertently devising our secular destinies placing themselves above God.

It is not easy to find the proper words to bring us together as a human race and Americans. So much has gone on in our lives that it is difficult to think out our options, understanding the larger personal responsibilities we have to ourselves. If too much detail is discussed our faces glaze over with information overload. That is why so much has not been covered in these chapters like global banking, world finance, drug interdiction and rehab, legal and medical reform. Yet, to move forward in what is being proposed, to reverse some of damage we have accomplished, the initial ingredient is to downsize our government's responsibilities to each of us then, minimizing the corruptive influences created by politics.

Future change of the magnitude being presented will require that all humans involved be intuitive, patient and inclined to listen well. If we are not able to recognize the need for this transition it is not going to happen. The Earth and our neighbors will strike out and back with the special interests groups becoming more fully ingrained in their power controls.

It will take a major leap of faith to convince America that she has major problems, and for our politicians to become willing to eventually relinquish the government's role in our parenting processes. Out of this, our current faith levels and human ingenuity will be continually tested in creating the vista of where we are and are going, and how we are eventually going to get there.

Each of us who embrace a need for alteration will also need to develop faith levels to weather the storms of our ingrained habits and walls of human resistance and fear of change. To sever the umbilical of our current conditioning with tough love, allowing us to grow together as humankind. In this, we will need to evolve in our confidence from within, to become more reliant on our inner spirit and the input of our Father. And to recognize that we have a pretty good chance to correct our past mistakes, short and long-term, once we decide the on the mission statement.

We will need to be willing to adjust our personal expectations of future government services. Personally deciding what we are willing to relinquish, then personally gain in this transformation.

The future objective is to revise our political domestic policies into a restructuring that will be user-friendly and managed in a compassionate manner. An estimated 41 cents of each tax dollar collected annually (700 billion dollars) and spent on these programs is misappropriated and misspent on pork barrel programs or stolen by insiders.

Using a debt free nation in the next 20 years would be a strong motivation to endorse this transition, as all future generations would benefit in this prudent reengineering. Like any child's first step taken, an initial suggestion would be to limit our national expenditures for our presidential race with true political reform.

1. Via public mandate, election spending can be held to one million dollars or less for each qualified candidate; monies supplied through the nation's treasury (to cover travel costs, communications and incidentals). This would alleviate the control of special interests groups, as all of our politicians voice complaints about the constant need for soliciting campaign money as their compromising issues. This factor would be eliminated. The immediate effect would subtract the need for each politician and political party to barter his or her personal ethics in this equation.

2. The cost of publicity and media coverage would be borne on a voluntary basis, falling under the realm of public information, encouraging town meeting forums with more televised and printed public debate. Statewide and local public office spending would be downsized proportionally following the lead of Washington, D.C. The networks and newspapers would have to sacrifice their present ad-revenue base derived from our current system, but all persons running for political office and the general public would have the immediate benefit.

The result would allow each candidate running for office to express their views of the "cause and effect" of each issue and how they would address the cause and not the symptoms. This, in turn, would provide the vehicle to allow the true positions of our many political parties to surface. We, the voting public, would be educated in this process to understand the scope of the social situations through the minds of each candidate and their grasp of local concerns; then we would be able to prioritize the magnitude of this Nations many growing problems.

3. As we are a nation driven by money we can relate to our largesse and waste and the need to simplify our tax systems. Over sixty percent of our current budget is allocated for social programming and interest payments, thereby creating our current financial and legislative challenges. The few political options touted are to cut services, or borrow more, or manipulate the tax base with new tax law. What is not being politically explored in general discussion is the current system of internal waste and abuse and their elimination; or the permanent, common sense and true bureaucratic downsizing of our government's internal operations.

With media development, a general path can be initiated, weighing the pros and cons while comprehending the benefit and loss before it happens. The General Accounting Office, the Inspector General's Office and a number of highly respected non-profit organizations have already identified programs that are outmoded, duplicative, and counter productive in managing the current bureaucracy.

Over 600 areas of government programs have been analyzed with common sense recommendations for fiscal reorganization and by running the country in the manner as a non-profit organization. Through these various studies, almost 4.5 trillion dollars of wasteful spending can be saved in the next five to seven years with programmed intelligent thought and revamping of government practices.

As identified by these study groups, the elimination of pork-barrel politics and the inefficiencies of our governing bureaucracies would generate approximately 360 billion dollars in saving annually. These savings could be optioned, with little human pain, against our nation's principle debt on an annual basis over the next decade. This, in tandem, would lower the borrowing cost for the average American.

4. By implementing these suggestions it can be anticipated that the annual budget could be reduced by more than seven percent each year. This step would initially place us on a positive path of economic stability in the long-term. It could also provide for a simplification of our tax systems leading into a deflationary stance on the tax structure by lowering, then negating, the need for a corporate tax across the board. A 20/20 flat tax could be introduced to Congressional Committee in the near-term… a simplified form of tax reporting of post-card size formatting.

The first $20,000 of the income of a family of four or $5,000 per person would be tax exempt. The tax rate would be 20% on the balance with the family responsible for their personal healthcare and retirement funding. By phasing in this program over a 5- to 50-year span, persons having more children than two would not benefit from having more babies. There would be no other form of personal deduction.

Business and corporate rates could be altered with an allowance of 20% of the taxes due, deducted for capital investment directly related to education, research, domestic development and environmental enhancement. These same incentives could also be placed on high mileage automotive R&D and for refurbishing the nation's existing structures rather than adding concrete in undeveloped areas.

This concept would encourage cluster development, clean transportation and density development and renovation with long-term investment in people and product. A 20% tax would be assessed on the balance of all of America's corporate gross profits until our nation's principal indebtedness is paid in full. After satisfied, the corporate tax would be eliminated for overall motivation.

This system would reduce our present complex system of auditing and streamline the accounting methods eliminating a positioning stance by manipulators of business numbers. Accountants, CPAs and tax lawyers would become the new employed by diversifying into monetary planning on a national and then, global scale. And if personally inclined, develop a phase-in, phase-out transition philosophy in the marketplace by using an analysis of our nation's and corporate companies' cash flow numbers following true general accounting procedures for future ethical and eco-friendly employment, and profit growth.

5. Phasing down government involvement in social programming over a 20-year period would lower the costs of inefficiency and reduce human despair. By shifting basic government services to privatization through price and values offered, competition would produce an annual budget requiring less than 700 billion dollars each year. The current complexity of tax law, spelled out in over 2,800,000 words (or 41,791 books this size), could be vastly reduced to but a few pages to be utilized. Government social activity would eventually be downsized and become more responsive to the country's citizens as the principle motivator with four oversight divisions.

Politicians and our government's bureaucracy would still have the responsibilities of regulating industry to keep greed at bay. They would also have the responsibilities of maintaining law and order, supporting the military and assuring the Constitutional rights of all the people they were elected to serve.

Our elected officials would have the oversight responsibility to assure that our country's social and ecological ills are being treated in a humane and compassionate manner. That medical and psychological service is available to all, at affordable prices with services provided by those who care about people. And that our children are being educated to think in a logical manner in much smaller classrooms mentored by teachers and parents who care about an education, and learn to treat others with respect, enhancing this country's future opportunities while restoring the childhood dreams we once had.

This planning will have to overcome our special interests' and our politicians' fears and their conditioned reflex of turf protection. By creating tax incentives in a 20/20 concept this transformation could save the Earth's resources, long-term, benefiting our families immediately. It could be pictured as a step-by-step process implementing the pieces together with cash-flow management and a productive citizen as its governing philosophy. If there were a re-thinking of why people think and act as they do, instead of a nation of separate interests looking out for number one, we could collectively become a united front looking out for each other.

6. The Internet, screen and newsprint would be the vehicles of this transformation with an overview of the "cause and effect" presented. Developing a vista that human lives are hanging in the balance, the result of our own decision-making processes could be the initial theme.

Quality persons could run for office without bartering their personal lives and values. This would attract capable persons from all areas of life, who would be able to share with the public their personal concepts for the future with solutions in a civil manner, explaining the how's and why's and their short and long-term costs. An evolution based upon logical reasoning, developing clarity and community understanding thereby creating a level-playing field.

The producers and directors could portray a picture of an America that is currently governed by a legislative mind that is boggled much like a juggling act. The average citizen today does not appreciate the mentality needed for basic city survival, as the existence of the inner-city resident is dependent upon one's "street-smarts", using the social system to personally survive. And that corporate America and their political action committees are doing the same thing in creating a non-productive service industry at a larger cost to this nation at large. It could provide the overview that the political element of this equation is confronted with fixing the reckless social programming of the 1960s to our present time. And to overcome the hard task that will hit us all, that our entitlement recipients, including our family members, will also have to experience becoming disenfranchised in this process of downsizing.

As a society we have the tendency to keep non-productive government programs and bureaucracy in place, to maintain a "status quo" that is costly and eventually self-destructive. Through this transition we will become family and neighborhood dependent as we used to be, creating a new generational mentality. We have a history of mastering the methods to destroy life. We now have the awesome task of mastering the requirements of saving it, by moving into the new requirements of the 21st Century then improving the world, globally.

One of the keys in moving forward is to have each one of us use our inborn talents, expertise and money to aid not only ourselves but all of us as equals in this world of God's. To recognize that each moment of life and what we have is a gift from our Creator and that it is okay to return some of what we have received. To step out of His way and allow Him to use us, and our positions to influence the thought and actions of others using our free will. And to recognize that this world's severe pains will need to be personally addressed by educating ourselves to accept His loving existence.

As each of us knows, there is nothing more gratifying than being approved by one's family and friends, and the positive effect and warmth it brings. Or being on the receiving end of a simple smile and hug of one's child expressing his or her love in a manner that is overwhelming. We are in need of a humane and compassionate vision with goals to strive for, to get going as a nation once again. There is an underlying internal and spiritual need to create something positive for our future tomorrows, with new rules for the individual game.

Today there are over 5,000,000 millionaires in the continental United States. More than 3,000 of these individuals own and control one (1) billion dollars or more, most having children. It is these persons and trusts/pension program managers who are often seeking a "profitable business proposition", a common sense corporate transaction with a positive return and light at the end of the tunnel. Most also want to be good parents. The above proposes a profit return and a legacy from our generation to theirs that will reward our personal and financial investment long-term for most, if not all of our grandchildren's lifetimes.

CHAPTER XVII
GLOBAL SENSITIVITIES

Around the 3rd century B.C. a graduate student of Aristotle conquered Macedonia. The empire at that time was believed to be the entire world possessing all the riches and wealth known to all of mankind. Before the age of 33, Alexander transformed this landmass into a spoke wheel of human enlightenment, based upon his intuition driven by his philosophical leanings. Under his guidance, two libraries were constructed in the inner part of this city to honor the teachings of his former mentors.

This community was to become a collecting magnet for all of man's knowledge gained since the beginning of recorded time. It is believed that this great megalopolis contained the complete published works and full texts of famous, and lesser known writers and historians, painting a picture of science, religious and philosophical understandings. The parchments, paintings and sculpted figures represented all the accomplishments and failings of man to the times.

This structure provided a chronological overview of where man had been and projected the potential of all that he could become — all housed in a centralized application of learning. Through the years this colossus transformed into a collection of international thoughts, ideas and life experiences. It also suffered from the lack of its leadership mentoring their following generations, providing long-range vision in accommodating change.

The period following Alexander's early demise left his people with an enlightened brief period of prosperity, which was then lost to human ignorance. This opportunity was transformed by religious zeal and Roman conquest, reverting benevolence into the carnages of rape, pillage and plunder, manifested by our human shortsightedness, with mankind again not appreciating what had been created. The energies of his visionary thought were consumed by man's greed and his ability to easily destroy.

The victorious military generals in dividing the spoils of war were not educated or sensitive enough to handle the responsibilities to continue Alexander's thinking or to settle their differences peaceably. The libraries' contents fueled the fires of the city's public baths until 650 A.D., leaving the economy and Alexandria in ashes. Over 90% of the city's libraries' contents were lost to political and financial posturing in dividing the spoils of war. What was gained through his young man's intuition, imagination and risk taking, having the potential to address the many problems of that era, resulted in a major devastation, with history again repeating.

The following generations did not know how to assimilate what they did not know, to continue his inroads of working together, passing on this knowledge to their children. We have been ebbing and flowing with mankind's advances and setbacks ever since, with the world's histories constantly repeating themselves.

Approximately 2,500 years later, in the early 1920s, the Earth's economy was geared to wartime industry production based on the borrowed dollar. Europe was in total chaos and ruins coming out of the throes of World War I. With the ending of this conflict, business volume was dramatically reduced; less people were needed for industrial production.

With the money drain of weapons and repairing the physical damage that all wars produce, the financial backers of this altercation accelerated their repayment demands. Germany was assessed the entire cost of the war incurred on all fronts. This in turn caused its financial collapse, leading into a domino effect, then depression throughout the world.

Few companies, and even fewer countries worldwide, were in the position to adjust their manufacturing methods into peaceful areas of production. Business, being what it is, and then cut back on employment on all fronts which created a downward spiral affecting the average worker on the street. With Germany's default, the instant demands of repayment by the financiers then resulted in additional governmental taxation on all fronts. The abundance of people no longer employed and unable to pay this assessment then created a slave-type, management mentality cutting overhead business expense. Low cost labor replaced the high wage earner as the new underemployed.

It took a wheelbarrow of money to buy a loaf of bread in Germany at the time. The value of the Marc in 1921, as the Greek coin in 391 A.D., and then rest of the world's currencies, was caught in a magnified downfall in worth from their original value. Financial bankruptcies in Germany led the world into a major World depression creating a new set of dynamics. During this period, a young Austrian who was a product of stern nurturing and an abusive housekeeper (taking her personal frustrations out on him with a broom), taught himself to manipulate the system for his personal revenge and political control.

Jewish bankers in their haste to collect on their loaned-dollar initiated a new set of unseen events leading into disastrous proportions of human response. By forcing his father, a small businessman, into bankruptcy, the stress on the family and this young man created the inner sanctums of anger and hate.

Hitler was able to use the correct timing of words to create a hope for his fellow man. He convinced his countrymen that he would be able to put food back on their tables if they would follow his lead. The result of these events soon came to the surface in lethal confrontations with Germany again taking on the world. With the financial backing of a handful of the same European families who underwrote the funding for the First World War, this young man was elected by a single vote. During his tenure over 60 million persons were killed as a result of history repeating itself in disastrous proportions, initiated by but a handful of persons caught up in their self-importance, their need for immediate gratification and myopic professional greed.

When one starts talking or thinking about the world's many problems the mind and attention span glazes over. Unless one is trained or inclined to delve into "cause and effect," history is of little importance to the average person. It is boring until it becomes personal and costly. For this reason, this chapter opened at a different time, leading to where we are today. Two stories of two different men living in different eras both exposed and conditioned by their early childhoods. One growing through his times, being educated to understand things on a much larger scale, educated to understand the much larger human vista and do something positive with his existence, but also losing his life much too early to have a continual impact. Showing us historically that no matter how much one has, or how successful they are, they will eventually leave it all behind. And another who could have had a tremendous positive impact on his fellow man, but because of the actions and reactions of his world as a child, was driven into a personal madness with a willingness to destroy all living things.

It is also two stories of two charismatic leaders not being educated to appreciate and build upon what they had, not learning from the mistakes of their predecessors, losing the opportunity to improve man's lot in life. Two stories of the rise, decline and fall of what could have been great foundations for our current world. With history again repeating we, like these two civilizations and historical eras, are again being tested as history's latest experiment in measuring mankind's adaptability in addressing his overall survival.

When President Gorbachov realized that his nation was being bankrupted by its military and political inefficiencies induced by the philosophies of Communism, he took a major step that went against his grain of professional conditioning. He could have maintained a status-quo position holding onto his status and power living in an isolated world of entitlements, but instead became willing to sacrifice his position to do what he thought was the right thing for his country and fellow men. He listened from within his heart to recognize that his country was being destroyed from within. He took a major leap of faith when he decided to educate his countrymen the need for dramatic change. He admitted governing failure.

Out of all of this, we in the free world are also in the process of learning about our governing failures and the need for immediate and dramatic change. We again are being challenged to either fix what we have in a peaceful benevolent manner, providing for our following generations, or we will repeat historical duplication. We can either do what we are doing adding to the many pressing dangers and confusions of our times, or we can get out of God's way and allow Him to work through each one of us.

We are now confronted in dealing with our own past errors caused by the lack of anticipation and a long-term focus of our nation and its problems with the rest of the world. We are now floundering with the sum total of all of our generations' decisions, personally seeking some level of sanity in an era going rapidly insane. Out of this we are in a spiritual and emotional process of deciding our path for our and our children's future survival. We are presently an unperceptive nation far removed from the realities of the rest of the world, a world now splintered and suspicious of our political and economic motivations. Many persons throughout this globe who harbor hate for us have suffered through atrocities we in this country can hardly imagine, let alone will ever totally experience. They see what we have, our materialistic possessions, as their personal expense.

Because of their extreme poverty and their leaders inability to see the world through our eyes, they have become conditioned to react in desperate terms for their and their family's immediate survival. Tens of millions of their children, who will be adults soon, are currently being indoctrinated not to love but to hate by these zealots who would like to see our eventual comeuppance and ultimate downfall. They are not being educated to appreciate our past and current efforts in this world, but instead perceive our disrespecting the value of all life originally designed by our Creator.

It is a foundation of allowing our world's generations to evolve into disrespect for themselves and others who will become increasing dangerous because of this conditioning. Their lack of hope and opportunity will soon drive their inner emotions, as they will make their decisions based on what they perceive to be the truth. In this country, a similar path is being duplicated for our children, and future generations following our footsteps.

Our youth today experience an adult world slowly chipping away at the moral fabric and foundations of what had previously provided the insight and sensitivity to generate this Nation's Constitution and Bill of Rights. What they see is a nation of corporate corruption and political incompetence with the inability to plan for a kinder and safer world. They know in their hearts and minds that the adult decisions driven by force, posturing and greed instead of compassion and peace are now laying the foundations of their future world, a world more confrontational, out of human control.

Until we understand and accept the many causes of our human conditioning and handle the acceleration of our times we, like Rome, will need a strong responsive military to protect us from the growing evils of this world. History has shown us that terrorism plagued Greece and later the Roman Empire for well over seven hundred years.

If we commit ourselves to allow God to lead us, we have the potential to break the back of historical duplications by coming together, living in World peace. We have the human ability by listening with our souls to create a world that two generations from now to where books will be written; movies directed and songs sung with a much different vent. Their messages would be the sharing of the unconditioned love for all of humankind.

By addressing our earthly differences with compassion and larger human understanding, communicating one on one on a personal level, we can bridge the world's current economic and spiritual divisions stressing humankind's commonality. To understand that each of the world's major altercations were originated by two persons seeing the same things differently at their inceptions, with one decision-maker being backed into the corner and then overreacting. And that each one of us can be reached on a deeper human level to develop solutions to the larger more pressing issue, the ecological health of this Earth. If we lose her integrity, no matter our ingrained habits and perceptions, we are gone.

Our generation and our following generations are being challenged to listen to our times, to grasp the mistakes of our political policies and reverse the tragedies of the world. And all through this, void the atmosphere of a major war to ever be created again. To undermine the factors that lead into armed conflict and human genocide, by recognizing that a person gainfully employed and loved is less likely to want to become a terrorist or a corrupted future leader.

****

Each elected official, compromised by political circumstance, ends up like the kid in a street gang not wanting to lose “face” or position of power. In this, the lines in the sand are often drawn, developing a “them vs. us” mentality separating us a human beings. With this comes the preconditioned perception that we will always be addressing the Earth’s many human altercations with belligerence and military might. Because of our domestic political ineptness, driven by money and our leadership’s hidden agendas we have been conditioned to believe that force will always be needed as a “supposed” last resort. It is far easier for them to use force and threat, than to diplomatically think out peaceful reforms.

Over the past four decades the United States has spent more than ten trillion dollars supporting our inability to develop a more compassionate world. We have the continued history of damage control, backed with a “crises management” mentality, which creates the need of spending hundreds of billions of dollars annually on the war machine for human control. We consistently react to those who oppose us with armed force and political threat, rather than invest far less in social and human education and human support programs around this globe.

We learned on September 11, that we do not have many of the answers to this world’s many disastrous problems as a single nation. We are being forced to recognize that our domestic corporate agendas and political posturing, in many instances, have caused our many divisions with much of world. With mans arrogance combined with each nation’s ignorance in world matters consistently surfacing; we hurt those who need our help the most, being led by those far removed from the needs of those being governed. It is, if we are inclined to think this out, a repetition on a global scale, of what the Roman Generals did to the citizens of Alexandria.

The United Nations, like all things over these past 50 years, has become mired in its own set of politics and human inefficiencies, losing site of its originating purpose. The U.N. was originally chartered to address and arbitrate the many injustices in this world; utilizing peer pressure, minimizing the need for military force. Franklin Roosevelt's intuitive vision, commitment and personal focus, which founded this entity, were lost with his death. The following generations of leadership in this country never fully embraced his philosophies of world order, weakening its importance.

In its governing Preamble, the U.N. was initially structured to save succeeding generations from the destructions of war, stressing the dignity and worth of the human person. It has the strong mandate to address global altercations with internal peacekeeping forces and supposedly its negotiating capabilities. In its attempts to protect and mediate the "real" and philosophical divisions of all nations U.N. membership many times becomes the victim of a "bull in the china shop" mentality. Certain nations band together with mutual "want and need", by creating a voting block, developing a turf protection mentality. Each strong element, those with the most resources including us, the United States, then becomes manipulative, wanting its personal political agendas to prevail over the sovereignty and collective issues of the rest of the world. Because of our inability to grasp the histories of all other nations, we attempt to financially sway or intimidate others into accepting our position. We, as example, will withdraw our membership dues or revert to military force or buy another nation's support, undermining the authority and importance of the U.N. which, if we seek world peace, is what we are challenged to reverse.

Almost 60 years ago, the Germans and Japanese learned well from what we taught them after the Second World War. Their later business success was the result of the Marshall Plan incorporating their individual expertise, thinking in broader and longer terms. They learned early on that it takes the combined effort of private business, managed by a farsighted visionary government and the educational system working together (with long-range goals) to be effective. With shared focus and clear vision they were able to overcome the costly mistakes of not planning for the eventual outcome. They operated under the philosophy and premise that when people feel confident about where they are going, that market forces will do well also.

Today all governments, on all levels, can likewise establish a socioecological program for the planet, by embracing the original philosophy and charter of the United Nations. Then incorporate the format structured within the Marshall Plan and Charles Deming's 14 Points for Excellence and to actually embrace the intent of the U.N. founders, whose originating intentions were to bridge the many gaps of our social divisions and repair the damages of human induced conflict. The United States can take the lead to use our wealth, benevolence and industry to create and then embrace, a broader long-term vision for each of us. Then by personal example, eventually influence the balance of this world.

Over 70,000 foreign and domestic projects that have been identified by the United Nations and the non-profit private sectors that could create immediate work in an overpopulated world undermining the results of poverty and human ignorance. Addressing these global needs would result in the long-term potential of offsetting the many inroads made by terrorist over the past 50 years. The start-up cost would be negligible, the world's infrastructure and future financing is already in place.

Today, as in our nation, localized graft, corruption and incompetence in each country keeps much of the world's aid away from those in true need of help. The weak are the pawns for the strong, and for that reason health and vocational programs should be planned on the local level bypassing corrupt governments. Through world pressure mediated by the U.N. and a nation's peers, an overall business and social plan can be developed for each country in need including one for the entire Earth; a plan mirroring, globally, what can be accomplished with man working compassionately with man.

Using immediate debt retirement for the Third World and tying in projected future income could become the prime motivators for the Earth's future global economy. Over 10 trillion dollars in private funding is available for domestic and international investment with a realistic return on capitalization. This could be administrated under the auspices of the U.N., the World Bank and International Monetary Funding to plan for then fund the repairing of this Earth. The retirement and pension funds both public and private could be matched dollar for dollar with comparable portions of the world's military spending in supporting this restoration plan.

By utilizing the human arm of this world body, UNESCO (educational, scientific and cultural organization) cottage industries in each of the world's townships and communities can become vested on the local level. The best and brightest talent of all the Earth could be utilized to educate the world's populations; and in turn, over the next three generations restore each nation's infrastructures, allowing each person the sweat-equity path of becoming self-reliant.

Through a humane thought process, this program at each level would be structured to produce a gradual 7% tax on all profits. This would generate a return on investment and be perpetually funded. With the U. N. administration expenses never exceeding 3% of the total monies generated, the balance of the collected revenue would be used to pay a negotiated percentage return to the investors.

With human practicality, we can eventually transform our current defense/war mentality into a global social and environmental business application as a secular motivation. In a well-developed concept for mutual benefit, with computer enhanced images, high speed and monorail systems, aqueducts and underground energy/filtration systems, and restoration of our and the world's forests, would sustain a lifetime of earning potential. A greening of our deserts for food production could create high levels of sweat equity and employment. Strategic and synergistic partnerships with all nations could be entertained including family and population planning, respecting each nation's sovereignty and the human rights that all should have as the children of our one God.

Bartering goods and sweat equity for outside services can be negotiated long-term, creating individual self-esteem on the local level working though local leadership. Private scholarships, grant monies and tax incentives could be awarded to individuals and groups developing the best cost-effective, comprehensive plans for each program developed. This would establish human creativeness as the priority.

The world's colleges, universities and Vo-tech programs could be challenged and rewarded for developing the well thought-out blueprints picturing a national and international program of continual human social improvement. Using common sense ethical business practices, employment can be created throughout the world with larger thinking from corporate management. Private industry driven by compassion and economics would then find the means to profit the planet with little government intervention. This, in turn, would allow each person and government the opportunity to create his or her future destiny on his or her own terms, becoming self-reliant.

CHAPTER XVIII
THE THINKING MIND

This electrical mass between our ears has the exceptional capacity to birth a thought or ideal. It creates a mental, then physical image with the capacity to induce change. It has a history of overcoming disastrous odds of defeat with answers of worth, becoming user friendly in its system of maturing. It is a tremendous tool when used and trained properly.

In our lifetime, we have seen tremendous gains and as noted, experienced many personal dysfunctions and self-created devastations. We live in a standard of existence envied by the majority of the world yet with a tremendous cost with what we have today. In this, we are pushing hard against universal energies, which are now pushing hard against us.

Each child who enters this life is a gift from our Father, full of promise and hope. Each little life brings a great potential for the future, providing for a continuation of the genesis of mankind. Every young soul is filled with an innocent inquisitiveness to create many miracles and move against what seems to many to be insurmountable odds. When a bullet destroys a child's life; or a once productive person to a drug overdose or an uncaring society there should be more than a temptation to change our internal motivational systems. Our future survival is, and always will be, dependent upon the firm grounding of our children being able to simply care and love without prejudice and hate.

In this country, and more so around the world, less than one child out of ten is brought up in an ideal existence of mother and father providing love and a guiding, nurturing hand. The typical crime offender in this country is a poor white or minority member with little formal education experiencing the absence of one or both parents. Seven out of ten of these inmates in this land of bounty, a nation under our one God, were abused as children and exposed to narcotics and drug warfare before the age of thirteen.

Nationally, almost one out of six kids brought into the world each year has parents who are addicted to drugs and are dysfunctional. The natural mothers are addicted to the welfare of others, unprepared for the responsibilities of single parenting, with the loss of self-esteem. Their natural fathers are not known by their offspring and oftentimes the mother, themselves abused as children. Almost one out of five of our nation's youth go to bed hungry each night, the mother and child, abandoned, in need of serious medical, financial and mental care. The childhood upbringing for our inner city's youth, with little choice, is joining a street gang for guidance and their personal survival.

This tremendous stress on all of our adolescents is created not by themselves, but by all of us not being responsible adults in their lives. What the spoiled, over privileged generation and our uneducated do, from what they are conditioned to do, will eventually end up costing us countless hundreds of billions of dollars, duplicating what we process over again.

We constantly repeat the trial and error methods of "on the job" parenting, addressing the various symptoms, not the original cause. Bottom line, we were never formally taught the responsibilities of marriage and human relationships, and the lifetime commitment it takes to siring our offspring.

The majority of case studies of people troubled with mental, emotional and neurotic difficulties result from us being born into our world by adults unprepared for the demands of being an adult. The vast numbers of robberies, rapes, murders, financial and personal debacles of greed and power control, and human abuse are founded to an adolescent's early childhood; and how they were nurtured as young people. These factors establish the destructive baggage, which eventually surfaces across our nation and our personal homes, causing our current anguish and pain, and corporate corruption.

We are now entering into a third generation of duplicating this process once again mirroring many, if not all of the mistakes each one of us made in our lives. Many children are now becoming adults and are frustrated and internally angry, looking for parental answers that are not there.

In writing these words, I think back to my childhood years, relating to the innocence of the period and the feelings I have today. While I will admit that what is being proposed is very idealistic bordering on Utopic, I believe that our Father would have nothing less from his children.

I come from a generation that still had teachers and adults who cared about my education and me as a person. This is still with me today.

This early impact, along with my inner thoughts is now surfacing in this dialogue about a world seen through the eyes of a child, sharing my many concerns with you as an adult. I am, like you, learning to look at my life and this world supporting our travels as a collective child of our Father. This is why "I am who I am today", as Popeye would say, still able to retain the innocence of just being a child having difficulties in dealing with this modern day. Still trying to make some sense out of what we have evolved into today.

Ideally a child is brought into this world with two loving parents offering love and attention with dual guidance. Female and male mentoring provide the ability to overcome obstacles, and to overcome the difficulties of maturing, eventually becoming a responsible adult. With few exceptions, there is a strong likelihood of transferring these qualities to the following generations when this happens. The wisdom and experience then passed on to the grandchildren ad-infinitum. A child places the parents and teachers on a pedestal in this process and trusts, cares and loves until a disastrous event teaches something otherwise.

When a child is nurtured by physical and emotional abuse, there is a good chance that when this person matures, the process is repeated with the next two levels of offspring. Once the parent-child relationship is breeched by an adult or a loved one, the person becomes hardened and skeptical towards his existence with the rest of the world. When a person is forced to do something against his or her will there is a normal response of rebellion. This is not being sensibly or actively addressed by our current human development systems, or understood by our politicians in creating any corrective educational transitions.

Public schools have evolved into implementing various educational programs based on theory to rectify matters, to teach the basics for state and national testing which results in a bland mediocrity of our educational foundations and us. National and state testing conformity does not recognize that not all children test well or are inclined to embrace a dysfunctional world filled with computers.

We presently process our human minds with methods that are standardized, not identifying our spiritual purpose in life and that each of us are born with a natural giftedness. This process has produced thousands of studies trying to remedy the morass of our present teaching methods with over a third of our youth quitting their foundations before graduation, bored with the methods presented.

Our school systems, including our colleges and universities, are not emphasizing how to just communicate and listen with compassion and human understanding. Nor do they do an adequate job of incorporating the personal involvement of the parents at the inception of a child's education. Schools have broadened their courses of study supposedly to keep up with America's universal needs, yet have gotten away from the basic human need of understanding ourselves as human beings, including the responsibilities of simply explaining what an education means.

Over the past 20 years of our lives over 2,500,000 books, websites, studies and articles have been written and produced about this plight with recommended social and educational reform. All consistently address the same problems and weaknesses and constant failures of our nation's educational programs of 40 years ago. All gloss over the harsh ignorance of our human natures and differing values of not wanting to be forced into doing something that we do not understand.

The educational community privately recognizes that the system is failing and highly politicized in nature, but is personally unable to develop an overall consensus in who, or what, to trust for its repair. This process of education's political mismanagement and political division produces complexity and a high level of wasted talents. The continuous result is that each family and our nation lose the larger human value of each child's existence. In a world of over 191 nations we rank 1st in spending, and 17th in the quality of our education, reflective of our continued governing incompetence.

Today, teachers are charged with implementing conflicting political directives in direct opposition to the needs of the child as the real mother and father have little time for parenting their children. Because of this, teachers are placed in the role of constantly having to prove their worth as surrogate parents, nurturing 30 or more adolescent lives daily.

It is ironic that these last 25 years have produced unbelievable technological advances by some very sharp minds, yet the general population has not been educated use this transference as a useful tool. More than 250 educational studies in the last 24 months have disclosed a paralysis and a high level of teacher frustration with the politics replacing their educational responsibilities. The system takes the best and brightest teachers in the classrooms and promotes them into educational management for higher wage benefits. This implants a mentality that administratively it is safer professionally to keep on studying the problems developing additional reporting methods, requiring more study, than fixing the inefficiencies.

The vast majority of politicians are not sensitive in understanding the complex role and the challenges of educating the mind to think, or a person to listen. The office holder cannot be held to blame, as education's responsibility is volatile and non-definitive. Yet they manage the system politically and financially, calling "the shots" for local implementations.

To institute any corrective change would incorporate political risks, as there is little chance of appeasing the differing emotional factions. The many laws and programs mandated are never completely thought out, and rarely address the basic need of the child and teacher in the classroom. Politicians are unable to comprehend the various corrective paths for educational reform as they are far removed from an instructor's reality. Today there are too many kids and now too many teachers in the classroom who just don't want to be there, the subject matter along with the processes, boring and thankless.

The teaching community is becoming overwhelmed by an individual's economic disparity, a child's drug addiction and attention deficit disorder and the new responsibilities of being an educator as the child's absentee parent. Presently, if a child fails it is the fault of the teacher, not the failure of the parenting system. This causes negative ramifications of wasted time and continual uneducated generations with parenting separateness a growing problem.

With the changing need and roles to handle the transition of jobs moving from the field to the factory, new skills were needed to industrialize America over one hundred years ago. John Dewey and a handful of others using the Massachusetts school system for initial guidance created the foundations of our current public school system in the late 1800s. Although theoretically and philosophically correct in principle, our educational systems were never structured to teach and sensitively develop each child's natural talents individually.

Our early childhood curiosity leads each of us to explore our environment, and tests the adults nurturing our lives. This interchange leads each person involved in this interchange, into the art of understanding and coexisting with each other, oftentimes, in a peaceful manner by reasoning out our differences with others.

There are those from our learned world of educational experts who deem that the first three years of life, including our 9 months of incubation, and the first four years of classroom involvement determine our lifetime attitudes towards education. When you think back to where you were at ten years of age you can realize that your early life experiences laid the foundations of your current thinking and who you are today. If the child's parents are taught the importance of education to the child during this stage, the child as an adult will, more times than not, repeat the same for their offspring.

If a child is educated to understand the importance of human life, allowed to mature at his own level and is told that he possesses a special worth; and then reinforced by the parent will lay the foundations that have the "real" potential to last a lifetime. Conversely, if that child is physically and/or mentally abused and told that they are of little worth they will eventually lose their confidence, their self-esteem, with the larger potential of endangering others. Most if not all of our suicides, mass shootings and child abuse become the finished product, which today includes domestic terrorism on a global scale.

The key to moving forward is to dramatically alter this plight, taking politics out of the equation, allowing the human spirit to prevail. To take all that is working and cost effective, allowing our children to develop into the productive souls that they are. Today there are some exceptionally gifted children who are making a huge difference in this shrinking world.

By thinking above our emotionally charged issues, we can take the best of what we have and incorporate it into a national privatized social (kids working with kids) mentoring program using the local talent we have as a nation. As long as expectations are realistic, the thinking long-range, explained in a rational manner, it is possible to change the system and be fair to all. Teachers, parents, the Pentagon and the private sector have many programs in place to correct the morass, if a method of having their voices and experience can be heard and mirrored throughout this nation.

By incorporating our nation's successful educational programs with the World's educational knowledge, centralized information and teaching centers can act as in concert as regional information clearing houses. Our local schools systems would be able to tap into all existing educational programs that have proven success. We can create a social rethinking integrating the not for profit, the religious and the private programs of education, modeled on the Pentagon's programs for its military children. This would create an educational highway linking businesses, academics and our government into servicing the mental development of each child and parent, and the general public.

By prioritizing the many pressing issues our universities, local school districts, libraries, colleges and media could be placed in the mode to fulfill this role immediately. When a vision is created from the top to allow it happen, all initial integration of talent and financing can be initially programmed similar to the startup of our space program.

There is little need to make it complicated, as many of the solutions have already been outlined. "A NATION AT RISK" (a publication that identified cause and effect with possible solution making almost 2 decades ago) and hundreds of similar publications can provide the outline for content and information transference. Each local success and failure would be measured utilizing key personnel to explain, train and delegate to others in a professional and compassionate manner.

The solutions and life experiences already in place through these many local programs can be emulated with each state and community learning from the successes and failures of each program. This would result in a nationalized clearing-house of knowledge, educating others to become efficiently productive. By using a hand-in-hand approach to teach public awareness, each educational success can efficiently and effectively educate other public systems in becoming self-sufficient, then privately managed.

It should be realized that our education is a key part of our life conditioning, affecting personality, civility in personal relationships, morals, work ethics and lifestyles. The primary purpose is to teach each person to analyze and question, and to know where to go to find and create answers. From this thought a curriculum can be devised to educate the parent, teacher and student to think logically, then to communicate and address life's challenges earlier in a child's life with intelligence applying common sense initiatives. An action plan creating a calendar of events, eventually developing an individualized program for each child and the natural parents. A regional then national adult program could be originated to do the same for our educators and politicians.

The curricula in the classroom could be developed, making reading, writing, mathematics, and foreign languages and teaching the responsibilities of parenting through grade nine. Morals, discipline and thinking can be implanted through out the program then become every day occurrences when we tire of our present ineptitudes. Incorporating past and present proven materials each of our natural mental gifts can be identified at the fourth grade level. From this assessment, individualized subject matter could then enhance the trained development of a child's interests.

The class load per teacher (excluding physical education) would be reduced to a maximum responsibility of 15 students per instructor. European and Asiatic methods and local successes could be additional models to be learned from and improved. Nine years of basics, including a thorough grasp of a second language. The student, parent(s), and teacher together then decide the strengths of a future vocation. The curriculum is then fine-tuned for the following three-year period.

Vocational and higher academic paths could be treated with equal respect, reward and appreciation with the right marketing approach. There could also be a planned interchange of company employees from the private sector, exchanging places with the classroom instructors, incorporating the various programs in existence. These cross-instructors would then understand and appreciate the challenges of teaching the mind to think, then become productive.

With an anticipation of knowing where our nation is planning to go, vocational and academic tracts can be accomplished with intelligent planning for future growth and job opportunity. There are desperate needs for artisans and craftsmen, medical and infrastructure repair and the simple need to grow non-polluted food. This entire process would eventually be financially underwritten using the nation's current budget for education and company retraining, and over the next three generations phasing out much of the overall costs of our judicial and prison systems.

By diverting and integrating part of what we legislate on federal, state and local levels (phasing out the expenditures over a 20 year period), instead of spending over $28,000 a year incarcerating a person, a proportionate dollar increase could be spent in educating each of our nation's young children. Additional funding and block grants could be solicited from civic and business groups with the community at large benefiting, with the student eventually becoming a responsible, productive adult. The income of the teacher would be increased to the comparable levels of responsibility of our private business sector. This format could eventually be applied on an international level, with implementation on the world level, eventually coming under the auspices of the United Nations.

The use of each community's present school system could be expanded to 12 months of use nationally, creating year round education and a more prudent use of our current facilities that would be cost effective. Where feasible, the small neighborhood school could be reintroduced, creating the spokes of a wheel with a mutually shared arts and science center acting as the hub. Neighbor can work with neighbor refurbishing dilapidated inner city and rural buildings, similar to an Amish barn rising and residential construction via the Habitat for Humanity programs rewarding sweat-equity involvement through scholarship rewards.

This process would incorporate our public and private sectors current expenses for education; to include the downsizing of the needless duplications of administrative bureaucracy and the financing of large school building systems housing 4,000 students or more. Inner cities and suburban settings would be able to offset approximately 30% of new construction cost with this "wheel and hub" approach and downsized with smaller neighborhood schools. Strip malls and empty office space could be utilized instead of being destroyed.

Parents and volunteers, through their personal involvement and sweat equity, would create a personal interest in each neighborhood's child, reinforcing the importance of community cooperation. Each dilapidated neighborhood could be reborn in this transformation by educating our children in smaller, more personalized facilities of instruction. In this, each participant and neighbor would be able to appreciate human value and get to know each other in the process gaining respect for each other. This would have the potential to alter the way we treat each other locally. When though out for the long lasting reward, this assimilation has the real potential of offsetting a large portion of the financial costs of our present penal systems.

On the world front, grants and scholarship funding to each local community could be introduced through the United Nations in conjunction with the World Bank, the IMF and other international financial and business institutions for eventual global implementation. There could be a quarterly overview of each local program's successes and failures with tracking the student's performance throughout the entire educational process. Each teacher involved would be rewarded financially. The eventual goal: An efficient, cost-effective and affordable means of transferring what is working to where it is needed and teachers earning a livable income. There could be an annual service fee established working on a generalized formula for fair compensation for the participants. Perhaps a $1.00 monthly assessment for each nation's citizens could be initiated for start-up capitalization involving each parent with a vested interest with the child gaining confidence and self-esteem on a global basis.

Our lives and activities from early adolescence to adulthood could be molded through perseverance, risk-taking, competitiveness and tough but compassionate love. Present and future politicians could be educated to open their minds, to assume responsibility and act in the best interests of the population thinking "we" instead of "me". Through electoral and political reform our country would have a chance to listen to our inner intuitions once again, when we learn how to do so.

By developing future graduates of good character and sound moral grounding, competence and responsibility would be the surfacing factor over the next three generations. The attitudes of the adult could be transformed with teachers promoted to levels of mastered excellence. The best and the brightest from the private sector can be utilized to compliment our present educational personnel. Persons can transfer experience and intelligence from the business, law and economic communities with an opened opinion, creating a light-bulb effect in each person's mind.

Emphasis could be placed on teaching teachers how to teach, administrators to administrate prudently, and politicians the corporate responsibility that comes with public office. To release their control of the educational system to those who know how to educate. And us to listen from within, growing through our childhood imaginations into a world of new possibilities.

This additional energy and practical experience could reawaken dedication and the commitment to excel. The involvement of the student, the parent(s), the teacher, the administrator, the private and public sectors working in tandem for the long-term.

In this transfer over this next decade, business manufacturers can learn to adjust their priorities and long-term cash flow, changing their goals from short-term profit taking and planned obsolescence, to manufacturing better and more affordable products benefiting their bottom line in the long-term. Employees can learn through training and retraining to produce quality merchandise and an honest day's labor for an honest day's pay. To be responsible for what they manufacture and service. Our governing and financial institutions can plan the development of a deflationary monetary program, having the necessities for human life made affordable again.

Churches can, with prayerful thought, become involved in developing a moral, human redirection for our individual spiritual nurturing; displacing our current secularized dogmatic positioning with the World's many religions. By embracing the mentality that we have but one single God, the many divisions we have as His children can eventually be overcome when we learn to personally accept each individual's path for spiritual growth. After all, each of us in our own special way is spiritually finding and developing who and what we are as His children.

CHAPTER XIX
IMAGINATION

I feel that my grasp of our English language is inadequate to explain all things distinctly enough to touch the souls in each one of us. I have tried to not be too critical and apologize for using the words “need”, “must” and “should” in reference to things we may eventually decide to do. That is for you and God and our future planners to decide.

So much of what you have just read has been already discussed and recognized by many of us, yet we seem to be hesitant to move beyond where we are at this present moment. This is part of our unspoken human nature, as it is not easy to formulate solutions that have the potential to be long lasting and far-reaching in their effect. Again, we are very good in making war and problems for ourselves. We are very poor in envisioning, then incorporating what needs to be done to create a better world; a World built with and containing human peace.

The great thoughts and intentions of our previous generations were diluted and lost with their deaths. They were not provided the apparatus to educate their contemporaries with compassion and a personal understanding, to continue the process they initiated — and to share their thoughts universally, which is something that we, as God’s children, are now challenged to correct.

We live in a period that is unique because it is causing a spiritual awakening. Combined with the Internet and its access we are being permitted to reach out to the entire world to overcome our miscommunication and work together. All the data, history and effective programs referenced in the previous chapters are available through this extensive resource to be used at our leisure for personal edification. By constructing a continual world road map incorporating a personal commitment for future generations to improve on, has the true potential to overcome many of our present calamities and impending global disasters.

I believe that we do have the human potential to accomplish these overall objectives and set goals together, if and when we get out of God's way and permit Him to move through each one of us; allowing His, not our, will to be done. And to realize that in our own special way we can influence each other in altering our reactive "me" instead of "we" behaviors. This can be formatted with an inner truth and realization that will have to relinquish our human controls to have a long reaching and lasting effect. The World's events and the negative energies of this era are seeking a benevolent and compassionate vision with larger thinking and much larger heart.

We are in the position to use our intelligence and concern and universal thought for this correction. If, in the future, we would personally envision a positive vista where our children and their future generations will benefit from our willingness to cooperate and sacrifice with each other, this single commitment and leap of faith would be the catalyst to ignite the positive energies of this world once again. When we open ourselves to allow this to happen, all is possible.

Our human existence is again being challenged to commit and recommit ourselves to the belief and existence of the Originator of our creation and allow His will to be done. And conversely grasp the concept that if we keep on doing what we are doing, we are the lemmings following our Pied Piper over the cliff.

As there is safety in numbers we will have to choose to move forward collectively, yet individually, in socially re-engineering ourselves in mapping out a positive journey for our future travels and spiritual growth. To establish higher priorities in each of our lives, understanding the events that affect the "who and what" we are as individuals; and then do something positive in each of our homes with this knowledge.

As mentioned, this book is just one of many vehicles that God is presently using to reach each one of us, to hopefully touch the inner spirit of our souls. Just a few suggestions and nudges, hopefully formatted in a less destructive manner than September 11, 2001, to have us see this world through the thoughts and concerned actions of our Maker. I also want you to know that this is just one of many person's attempt to open our thought process, to "jump-start" a major adjustment to what we are doing to ourselves.

Each of us is now charged spiritually to obtain an understanding of human life and one's role of caring for each other, eventually evolving into an unselfish, unconditional love. The result has the true potential of creating a fulfillment with a definite purpose. The causes of our individual stresses will be lessened, a smile coming easier. The outcome of this effort will result in an explosive personal growth, establishing each of us — you, me and everyone else — to be caring children for God's wonderful world.

When the individuals leading each nation's evolution and business management understand the total scope of our impending future, we could become mutually educated to address our times as God's children. We together can use our collective inborn intuitive intellect and human spirit in this total endeavor staying out of His way.

I again ask that you place this into prayer. Then listen to what your heart and intuition tells you. Then walk in absolute faith. The next few years of our lives can make a vast difference. That is for you and our God to decide. I believe He is right here waiting for us to get our act together and then to listen to His loving presence and concerned direction. He wants to be utilized.

****

Picture the future with a cold March day refreshingly clear and crisp. The sun is shining brightly through high billowing cumulus clouds. The atmosphere is giving the gentlest hint of spring, a period of a burgeoning green, foretelling summer's abundance.

The use of artificial chemicals for the nation's food supply has been discontinued, replaced by organic nutrients. Farmlands and property use are in the mode of being intelligently developed, adhering to the basic requirements of the land. Small farms managed by individuals who enjoy the labor of creating uncontaminated food for our nation's supermarkets. Urban and suburban landscapes are sensitively planned, with lowlands, marshes and forests being naturally restored. The percolation systems with natural filtering properties produce clean drinkable water. Nature is afforded the time to digest and replenish the important nutrients for man's survival.

All people are now sharing the ecology with an intuitive, intelligent sensitivity. All forms of life are now in cooperation for mutual benefit, cohabitating the Earth and restoring it with renewable resources. Mankind is using its intelligence to reproduce what was originally intended.

Supply and demand is the marketing rule. Past methods of government subsidies and legal intervention are eliminated, lowering the nation's spending habits and tax needs. A deflationary system is incorporated into the economy, driving down the past period's artificially induced inflationary spiral. Goods and commodities are available, with prices remaining relatively stable year round. Government law making is now implemented with corrective measures to assure the long-range success of man's evolution thinking in the long-term.

The business communities' financial backers are now involved in the system conditioned for a continuous evolution. Sensible, intelligent elected leadership from all walks adhere to the simple guidelines of the Constitution and Bill of Rights, the judicial process and legal interpretations simplified to the adherence of God's Ten Commandments. In essence, people need less to purchase the basic necessities of life.

There is an ongoing analysis of the traditions, heredity and conditioning of the populace. Policy makers are now committed to maintaining human compassion when addressing life's challenges. The goal is to produce a population with the emotional capacity to understand the need of its immediate neighbors, each person now personally responsible for developing his and her future destiny.

Efforts of the media are now concentrated on effective communication and quality education. Beliefs and ideas of the general public form in-depth programming of cause and effect, with suggested remedies, via the 50-year plan established two decades before. With the advances in the technical and scientific worlds, machines replace the need of heavy human labor, a process mandating radical educational reform.

Man's time is spent utilizing his inborn mental abilities to grow and prosper. Education is given the highest priority, instrumental in society's moral alterations. People are now humanely interacting with each other. There are no divisions in the religious structure.

A person's natural strengths are developed, overcoming and compensating for one's inherent weaknesses initiated from the times of early birth. The varying mental, physical and emotional gifts are constantly being identified within each individual. The family unit living together in love is to be the continual product. An evolved system enriching one's life gives a sense of purpose and value with human aspirations and successes only limited by the reaches of the growing mind. No longer is a person's worth judged by his material possessions, but by his or her peaceable accomplishments in dealing with the needs of others.

Persons historically considered handicapped are positive contributors and producers, working with personal satisfaction, while gaining the approval of others. There were new methods of human intervention developed, re-enforced by positive common sense purpose in an era that affords the trials and tribulations of living, yet affords the potential for practical solutions to continually surface on all social matters.

Intuition's inner voice is the basis of human morality and the decision-making processes, its existence dependent on each person's inner spirit of energy and faith and the renewed ability to simply listen. All persons of all nations exist in peace without infringing on the beliefs of others. There is no conflicting interpretations of God, but a single concept of one benevolent Creator. It is the world of 2100 A.D., a world of compassion, love and human understanding. Perhaps a period envisioned by God when He created us.

And His planet,

Earth.

Your comments, feelings and suggestions are welcomed. I can be contacted via snail mail at P.O. Box 1574, Mt. Dora, FL 32756. Thanks, Bill Geringswald

References, research sites and additional reading for *A Child's Legacy*

Statistical Data

Learning From Data: An Introduction To Statistical Reasoning. Arthur M. Glenberg. Lawrence Erlbaum Associates: 1995.

U.S. Census Bureau (www.census.gov)

Statistical Abstract Of The United States U.S. Census Bureau: 1970, 1980, 1990 and 2000.

U.S Bureau Of Economic Analysis

World Population Profile Thomas M. McDevitt. U.S. Census Bureau: 1998

Fortune Global 500 L. Klema: 1995. (www.geocities.com)

Eurostat (www.stastics.com)

International Trade In 2000 (www.uaw.org)

World Trade Organization (www.trade.com/stats)

Global Financial System Lothat Komp. Executive Intelligence Review: 2001.

Bureau Of Economic Analysis

U.S. Dept. Of Commerce

Global Economics (www.zmag.org)

Trade Data (www.fas.usda.gov)

The State Of Working America Economic Policy Institute

Political And Financial Information Resources

A History Of Money From Ancient Times To The Present Day Glyn Davies. Rev. Ed Cardiff: University Of Wales Press: 1996.

The Wealth Of Nations. Adam Smith. (www.bibliomania.com)

"Debt Crises-Financial Leaders Endorse Debt Plan." Martin Crutsinger. Assoc. Press. 9/28/02.

"The Asian Financial Crises." Jeffrey D. Sachs & Wing Thye Woo. Harvard Institute For International Development And University Of Ca @ Davis: 1999.

"Forbes' Richest Americans Get Poorer." Rebecca Gomez. Assoc. Press: 9/15/02.

The U.S. and World Poverty. Wm. L. Furlong, Joan H. Joshi, Donald L. Plucknett, Nigel J.H. Smith, E. Boyd Wennergren. Seven Locks Press: 1989.

The American Encounter: The United States And The Making Of The Modern World. (Foreign Relations). James F. Hoge. Basic Books: 1997.

"Governments End: Why Washington Stopped Working." Jonathan Rouch. Public Affairs: 1999.

The Interest Group Connection: Electioneering, Lobbying & Policymaking In Washington. Paul S. Herrnson, Ronald G. Shaiko, Clyde Wilcox, Editors. Chatham House Publishers: 1998.

Improving Governments Performance: An Owners Manual. John J. Diulio, Gerald Garvey, Donald F. Kittl. Brookings Institution: 1993.

Disarmament And Development: A Global Perspective. Pradip K. Ghosh. Greenwood Press: 1984.

Technology And Industrial Development In Japan: Building Capabilities By Learning, Innovation And Public Policy. Akira Goto & Hiroyuki Odagiri. Oxford University: 1996.

www.questia.com

Ecological Issues

State Of The World 2000 (www.worldwatch.org)

www.villageorpillage.org

www.earthshare.org

Department Of Energy-Task Force On Strategic Energy (www.seab.energy.gov)

Ecoscience: Population, Resources, Environment. Paul R. & Anne H. Ehrlich. W.H. Freeman Publisher: 1977.

Global Dumping Ground: The International Trafficking In Hazardous Waste. Bill D. Moyers. Seven Locks Press: 1990.

"Perhaps No U.S. Streams Unpolluted." John Heilprin. Assoc. Press: 9/27/02.

Virus Hunting: Aids, Cancer And The Human Retrovirus. Robert Gallo. Basic Books: 1991.

"The Measurement Of Environmental Resource Values." A. Myrick Freeman. Resources For The Future: 1993.

The Third World In Global Environmental Politics. Marian A.L. Miller. Lynne Rienner Publisher: 1995.

Managing The Environmental Crises. Daniel H. Henning, William R. Mangun. Duke University Press: 1999.

Insurance Council Of North America

The Road From Rio. Thomas W. Dichter & Julie Fisher. Praeger Publishers: 1993.

Waste To Energy In The U.S. T. Randall Curlee, David L. Feldman, Michael P. Kelsay, Susan M. Schexnayder, David P. Vogt, Amy K. Wolfe. Quorum Books: 1994.

Protecting Natural Resources (www.johannesburgsummit.org)

Climate And Global Change (www.agu.org/sci)

Billions & Billions. Carl Sagan. Random House: 1997.

Black Dawn Bright Day Sun Bear with Wabun Wind. Bear Tribe Publishing: 1990.

A Sand County Almanac Aldo Leopold. Oxford University Press: 1949.

Thoughts From Waldon Pond. Henry David Thoreau. Pomegranate Communications: 1998.

River Of Lakes. Bill Belleville. University Of Georgia Press: 2000

Education

United States Department Of Education (www.infoplease.com)

U.S. Educational Studies (websearch.cs.com)

Digest Of Educational Statistics, 2001 (www.nces.ed.gov)

Schooled To Order: A Social History Of Public Schooling In The United States. David Nasaw. Oxford University Press: 1979.

Approaches To Cognition: Contrasts And Controversies. Terry J. Knapp, Lynn C. Robertson, Editors. Lawrence Erlbaum Associates: 1986.

Public Education Encyclopedia Of American Social History Vol. 3. Charles Scribner's Sons: 1976.

National Center For Educational Statistics

www.cwa-union.org Federal Communications Commision Nsd File No. W-P-D-443

Deming's 14 Points For Management (www.chuck.agsci.colostate.edu)

Mental Health And Legal Resources

Bureau Of Justice Statistics Aug. 1995

Hierosgamos (www.hg.org) (Legal Research)

Internet Legal Resource Guide (www.ilrg.com)

Family Violence Statistics (www.soundvision.com)

National Archive Of Criminal Justice Data

OSHA On Workplace Violence (www.pimall.com)

"Mental Health United States 2000 U.S Dept. Of Health And Human Services." Edited By Ronald W. Manderscheid, P.H.D. & Marilyn J. Henderson, M.P.A. (www.mentalhealth.org)

Philosophy

The Politics Of Character Development: A Marxist Reappraisal Of The Moral Life. Kit R. Greenwood. Greenwood Press: 1994.

Alexandria (www.ce.eng.usf.edu)

General Philosophy (www.xs4all.Nl)

Religion

The Bible

The Koran

The Torah

The Major World Religions (www.omsakthi.org)

The Peace Abbey And The Life Experience School (www.peaceabbey.org)

"Get The Most Out Of A Charity." Eleanor Laise: 2001. (www.smartmoney.com)

Reason For Hope. Jane Goodall with Phillip Berman. Chivers Press Bath, England/Warner Books: 2000.

Mutant Message Down Under. Marlo Morgan. Harper Collins:1991.

Religions Of The World. Lewis M. Hopfe/Mark R. Woodward. Prentice Hall: 2000.

A Road Less Traveled. M. Scott Peck/Morgan Scott Peck. Simon & Schuster: 1997.

How To Know God. Deepak Chopra. Three Rivers Press: 2000.

Conversations With God. Neale Donald Walsch. Hampton Roads Publishing Company, Inc.: 1998.

The Way To Freedom By The Dalai Lama. Harper San Francisco: 1994.

Many Lives, Many Masters. Brian L. Weiss M.D. Simon & Schuster: 1988.

Life And Teaching Of The Masters Of The Far East. Volumes 1-6. Baird T. Spalding. Devorss Publications: 1924, 1937.

General

The Peter Principle/The Peter Prescription. Dr. Laurence Peter. Bantam Books/William Morrow&Co. N.Y.: 1972.

The Art Of Negotiating. Gerard I. Nierenberg. Barnes And Noble Books, N.Y.: 1968.

Notes To Myself. Hugh Prather. Real People Press: 1970.

Profiles Of Genius. Gene N. Landrum. Prometheus Books Buffalo, N.Y.: 1993.

The Icarus Paradox: *How Exceptional Companies Bring About Their Own Downfall*. Danny Miller. Harper Business: 1990.

Animal Farm. George Orwell. Harcourt Brace Jovanovich, Inc.: 1946.

Grapes Of Wrath. John Steinbeck. Penguin: 2002.

Captains And The Kings. Taylor Caldwell. Ballantine Books: 1972.

Fire In The Lake. Frances Fitzgerald. Vintage Books: 1973.

Megatrends. John Naisbitt. Warner Books: 1982.

Stupid White Men. Michael Moore. Regan Books Harper Collins: 2001

Printed in the United States
24985LVS00006B/117

9 781592 862443